Journey Through

Thinking About Drinking

Towards a Safer Relationship with Alcohol

Stuart Linke

First published by Muswell Hill Press, London, 2012

www.muswellhillpress.co.uk

British Library Cataloguing in Publication Data
Linke, Stuart.
Thinking about drinking.
1. Drinking of alcoholic beverages—Health aspects—
Popular works. 2. Drinking of alcoholic beverages—Social
aspects—Popular works. 3. Alcohol—Physiological
effect—Popular works. 4. Alcoholism—Prevention—
Popular works.
I. Title
613.8'1-dc23

ISBN-13: 9781908995018

Printed and bound in Great Britain
by Marston Book Services Ltd, Didcot, Oxon

Acknowledgments

My first experience helping people with alcohol problems was as part of my clinical psychology training at Leeds University. Shortly after qualifying, I was struck by the number of people I came across in my work who drank heavily, so I invited Dr. Robin Davidson (now Professor) from the Leeds Addictions Unit to train a group of health service staff to develop a treatment service. He introduced us to the 'Drinkers Check Up' approach and helped us set up a service for problem drinkers at Pontefract General Infirmary in West Yorkshire. Whilst at Pontefract, I was invited to assist in founding a new voluntary service for alcohol counselling called Alcohol Services Pontefract and Wakefield (ASP&W). It was a volunteer at ASP&W, Charles Elstone, who had the original idea of developing a new type of self-help manual, based around the concept of a weekly treatment approach, which he created with the assistance of health education expert Toni Brisbee and some involvement from me. The manual was financially supported by a grant administered by Alcohol Concern and named by Charles and Toni 'Down Your Drink' (DYD).

The translation of DYD into a version suitable for the internet and the ensuing research programme was financially supported by the Alcohol Education and Research Council and the National Prevention Research Initiative hosted by the Medical Research Council. The intellectual support and enthusiastic encouragement came from Professor Paul Wallace of University College London who introduced me to Dr. Elizabeth Murray who had established the E-health unit, also at UCL. I am grateful to both for their guidance and friendship throughout. None of this work would have been possible without the agreement, interest and encouragement of my employers, Camden and Islington NHS Foundation Trust, including my colleagues in the psychology department.

The DYD research programme required that the content and design of the intervention be enlarged and improved. Special thanks go to Dr. Jim McCambridge and to Dr. Zarnie Khadjesari who both contributed much to the content and overall design.

I was originally approached by Mark Chaloner and Tim Read of Muswell Hill Press to write a book on a different topic from this one. It is a tribute to them that they were bold enough to accept the idea for this book and encouraged me to write. This book, although based on the original ideas in DYD, contains much that is different. A book designed to be read is different from a website that is created to look at and to navigate through. There is a great deal of new and original material in this book, including medical and health information, theoretical background and case studies.

The case studies are all inventions written specifically for this book. However, it is highly likely that fragments of real events and lives have found their way into the accounts. This was not intentional and I don't think that anyone reading the accounts would be able recognise themselves or someone they know in the stories. It is my experience that many people who drink a lot can be good storytellers and, given the right environment, may be happy to disclose personal information about themselves. The collective effect of having heard so many stories has been, hopefully, to enrich this writing and including them may assist readers in relating this material to their own lives.

My thanks to everyone who has assisted along the way. In the course of this book, when expressing ideas I have used the plural pronoun and said 'we' rather than 'I'. I chose to do this to convey my sense of a consensus among colleagues (practitioners, policy makers and researchers) about how risky and harmful drinking should be approached. This book has only one author, however, and any errors of omission or commission are mine alone.

Stuart Linke
June 2012

Contents

Table of Figures

Introduction

Excessive drinking probably does more harm than you think. It harms society, harms families and it may be doing harm to you. But you might not be aware of it. Recognising that drink is a problem is often not an easy process. Most people see some good things about their drinking and some bad things, and weighing up the pros and cons is a tricky thing to do. The aim of this book is to help you do this and then decide if you need or want to change anything about your drinking. There will be some case studies, some quizzes and lots of information to help you decide what is best for you and the people around you. The book will also help you think about if now is the right time to make some changes and, if so, to stick to the changes that you make.

It seems that society may be going through a big change in habits around drinking. People have always drunk alcohol. It is a tribute to the inventiveness of the human race that we have managed to turn all sorts of things into an intoxicating drink. Fruit, vegetables, grains — you name it someone somewhere has had a go at transforming it into something interesting and alcoholic. We do this because we like the taste and, most importantly, because we want the effect that alcohol has on us. This book is not saying that alcohol is bad. But, as a society, we are changing the way we drink and that might be quite a problem. We used to buy our alcohol in taverns and pubs (or sometimes make it at home), but now we buy it mostly in supermarkets. Despite government controls on advertising and price, the alcohol industry effectively targets us to increase our consumption. There are more women drinking regularly and they are consuming more than in the past. Binge drinking is a growing problem and young people are 'pre-loading' — that is, drinking cheap alcohol at home in order to get drunk before going on a night out. Alcohol is easily available and underage drinkers have few problems buying cheap booze, or getting served in licensed premises, using fake IDs purchased through the internet.

The effect on society of excessive drinking is truly staggering. Surveys suggest that between twenty and twenty-five percent of the adult population in the UK are drinking at levels that increase their risk of harm. And the harms are risks of developing cancer, liver disease, digestive disorders, heart problems and stroke, harming babies in the womb, having accidents and a whole range of different mental health problems. It is implicated in family breakdown, court appearances, loss of productivity and public disorder.

The European Union (EU) is the heaviest drinking region in the world, with each adult drinking an average of 11 litres of pure alcohol each year. A study published by doctors in *The Lancet* reported that nearly four percent of all deaths in the world can be attributed to alcohol misuse. The General Household survey in England in 2001 identified 6.4 million moderate to heavy drinkers and 1.8 million very heavy drinkers. Those figures have probably risen in the last ten years. (To find up to date news about alcohol related topics the BBC is a good source of information — you will find it at http://www.bbc.co.uk/search/news/alcohol. Specialist information is available from the US National Institute of Alcohol and Alcoholism (NIAAA) at http://www.niaaa.nih.gov.)

But facts and figures don't change behaviour. Telling someone, or telling yourself, to drink less isn't enough to make a helpful change. In fact, stopping drinking or cutting down may not be a problem. It is sticking to it that is difficult. As the old joke says, 'stopping drinking is easy — I have done it hundreds of times'.

This book is based on psychological research. Some of the research is about what motivates people to drink and why they may find it hard to control it. Other research is into the treatment of people with alcohol misuse disorders. This includes several different types of therapy supported by scientific evidence. These are motivational enhancement therapy, cognitive behaviour therapy, social and behaviour network therapy and relapse prevention. The same approach has been adopted in the 'Down Your Drink' website, which was designed by a team led by the author of this book. The website (www.downyourdrink.org.uk) is free to use and covers much of the same material.

Social attitudes towards drinking are mixed and can often be contradictory. Alcohol is promoted energetically as something that is cool, ordinary and fun. Alcohol producers, alcohol sellers and the licensed trade have a joint interest in selling us alcohol. People are sometimes proud of how much they drink and can talk excitedly about wild nights out — especially when they are young. Or having expensive drinks can be an outward symbol of how successful you are. Drinking can be a good way to relax after a hard day at work or an easy way to socialise with friends. It can help you to get things off your chest or make you more confident when you might otherwise feel nervous, such as when approaching strangers or people you feel sexually attracted to. It can make you feel powerful. In these ways alcohol can play an important and even useful role in people's lives. But drink too much (and behave badly) and society soon disapproves. Heavy drinkers can be blamed for all kinds of problems such as ruining town centres, filling up hospital beds, wrecking the economy, violence, crime, destroying families and loss of productivity. And there is some truth in these claims. But when society blames people the natural reaction is for heavy drinkers to hide away. So we have secret drinkers or people who disguise how much they consume. They can hide their drinking from themselves and hide it from other people.

The messages that come out of government bodies (in whichever country and from whatever government) can be confusing and difficult to interpret. The advice given usually refers to standard drinks (which vary according to country) and how many standard drinks it is considered safe to consume in a specified period of time. The recommendations are usually about how many drinks it is reasonable to consume in typical week. The information given is inevitably general — so much for a typical man (say 21 units) and so much for a typical woman (say 14 units). Of course, when we think of applying this to ourselves it is tempting to decide (mistakenly) that this general advice doesn't apply to us. Somehow we feel we are different. We may wrongly think of ourselves as having some kind of immunity. Perhaps we reassure ourselves that we are OK because we regularly go to the gym, eat healthily or have surviving relatives who 'could really put it away'. Often people look at the recommendations made by government departments, or official health organisations, and think to themselves that these guidelines are very low. If you have found yourself thinking along these lines, it may be worthwhile taking a good look at the issue and checking out some facts. This is one of the things that this book will help you to do.

The history of public concern about drinking is not very glorious. Too often there has been a moral and judgmental attitude from those in authority. Think of the nineteenth-century temperance movements and prohibition in the United States. There are well known sayings such as the 'evils of drink' or 'drink is the scourge of the working classes'. This climate has strongly influenced the way those who drink too much have been thought about. For a long time those who were dependent on alcohol were seen as having a disease called alcoholism. Alcoholism was viewed as fixed thing and it was believed that the only solution for these people was to be completely dry and never drink again. While this is true for some people, we now know that there are many people for whom this is not true. When a new psychological approach and treatment called 'controlled drinking' was introduced in the 1970s and 1980s, the researchers who developed it were accused of fraud and there was a very public row about it (see chapter 10). Fortunately, that is now behind us and some more useful terminology is in use.

Hazardous drinkers are those who drink more than the recommended limits. *Binge drinkers* are those who drink twice the daily limit in a single session. *Harmful drinkers* are people who drink more than the recommended units and are beginning to experience harms from their drinking. *Dependent drinkers* are those who feel they cannot function without alcohol and alcohol plays an extremely important role in their life. It is possible to be physically and/or psychologically dependent on alcohol.

If you think you may be dependent on alcohol then it is vital that you see a doctor before making any changes to your drinking. You will need a health check. Sudden withdrawal from alcohol can be fatal.

Personal reasons for thinking about drinking vary a great deal. Some people will be bothered by health worries. Others will be short of cash. In other cases it is comments from family or friends that provide the prompt. As we get older we begin to take a view on what is important in our lives and might reflect on what place we would like alcohol to have. The growing number of young professional women who drink heavily may be concerned about how alcohol is damaging the way they see themselves and perhaps the way others see them.

This book is for people who are willing to commit themselves to taking a serious look at the role alcohol plays in their lives and possibly getting to grips with a real challenge. The overall approach adopted is harm reduction. There are three parts to this book. Part One is called 'It's Up to You' and is designed to help you decide whether *your* drinking is a problem or not and whether you want to do anything about it. If you do want to change, this part can help you to decide what you want to change and if now is a good time to change. Part Two is called 'Making the Change'. This helps you put your plans into action and has ideas about how to best make the change work. Part Three is called 'Keeping on Track' and is about the rest of your life. It is about how to keep drinking at safe levels if that is the right thing for you, or not drink at all if that is your choice. It is about the likely pitfalls and how to overcome them.

PART 1

It's Up to You

CHAPTER 1

Are You Drinking Too Much?

Most of us drink. Some of us drink more regularly than others. But how often is too often? And how much is too much?

The fact is alcohol affects all of us differently. What is manageable for some can be a problem for others. If you are drinking regularly that may not mean you have a serious drinking problem but you could be putting yourself at risk of harm. It may only take a small change to make a big difference.

Let's start with a few case studies to set the scene and to stimulate some thinking. None of the individuals described in this book are actual people, although the stories are based on realistic situations and stories. The details have been changed to protect the identities of the people concerned.

Henry's Story

Henry started drinking at a young age. His parents always had a fully stocked drinks cabinet and they enjoyed wine with their meals at weekends. His parents would give him a taste from their glass and, by the time he was in his mid teens, he was sharing a bottle with them about twice a week and a couple of bottles on special occasions. At Christmas, birthdays and at celebrations, the bottles of spirits would come out and he enjoyed that. His parents were sociable and they liked to offer their guests a drink (or two). As he grew older, Henry began to drink beer with his mates after playing football (once a week) and after working out in the gym (usually twice a week). In his late teens he would go to the pub three or four times a week and at weekends hit the clubs in town, lose count of how much he drank, and would wake up the next day with a sore head. However, he was easily able to get on with whatever he had planned for the day. Henry started living with his girlfriend in his late twenties and stopped going to the pub as often. He had a good job and liked to stay at home and share a bottle of wine most weekday nights. At weekends they'd meet up with friends and have a few shots as well.

Does this seem like excessive drinking to you or normal? Can you work out how much Henry is drinking these days? (Don't worry if you can't as we explain how to do this in chapter 2.) Is Henry's drinking likely to be detrimental to his health (or his wealth)?

This would be a good moment to think about these questions. There are no right or wrong answers, but it will help if you can start pondering these types of questions so you can think about your own drinking in context.

The story moves on:

> After a couple of years the relationship between Henry and his girlfriend becomes a bit strained. There's nothing unusual about this and they cope with it by giving each other a bit of space and spending more time with their old friends. Then his girlfriend's mother becomes ill. She has breast cancer and all the family are worried. His girlfriend is worried about her own situation so she goes for a scan and fortunately she is OK. But her mother is not OK and has to have surgery and then radiotherapy. His girlfriend starts to spend a lot of time at her mother's house and doesn't have much time for Henry. Henry's job is now under threat. The recession is affecting his company and he needs to spend more time at work. After work he doesn't come straight come home, but goes to a wine bar with some colleagues and then occasionally a nightclub afterwards. When he comes home, his girlfriend is already asleep and at the weekend she is at her mother's house, so he goes to the pub and drinks heavily all afternoon on a Saturday and sleeps in on Sunday mornings. For Sunday dinner he eats at the pub and has a few beers. Over time Henry becomes depressed, his sleep is poor and he can no longer be bothered to see his mates. He drinks at home most days.

What about now? Does Henry have a drink problem or not?

> Six months later the news is better. His girlfriend's mother has finished her treatment. She is in remission and the doctors are hopeful about the future. Work is still a worry, but the company has a plan to cope and Henry feels there is a future for him with them. The couple resume their old habits and spend the evenings at home, but they are thinking about the future plans and just drink a couple of bottles of wine over the weekends.

What do think now about Henry's drinking?

Here is a different example to be thinking about:

Sian's Story

> Sian is twenty-three, single and living in a flat share with three girls. She thinks of herself as a moderate drinker and in control of her consumption. All the other girls in the flat drink and there is usually an open bottle of white wine in the fridge, and she will have a couple of glasses every so often. She doesn't count the number of glasses and nobody asks her, so she is not sure how much she drinks. Last Friday night Sian had a bit of a binge. It started around 6.00pm after work. She met a few friends for a drink during 'happy hour' at a local wine bar. Then she went home to get changed and to set off

for a club. At the flat she drank a bottle of cider bought from the corner shop on the way home. She felt that she needed a bit of confidence that night as there would be some guys she knew at the club and she normally felt shy in their company. She was determined not overdo it, though, as she didn't want to lose control or put herself in a risky situation. She met her friend at the entrance to the club and went inside. Her friend went straight to the bar and, as it was still early, the drinks were half price (for the girls at least). As the evening went on Sian found it harder to control her alcohol intake. The music was loud, it was crowded, hot and there was nowhere to sit. She kept drinking until she felt sick. She rushed to the toilet and threw up. Her friend was in a similar state to Sian and they decided to leave and look for a taxi to go home. It was at this point that Sian realised that she couldn't find her bag which contained her cards, purse and phone. Her friend said that she knew someone who lived locally. They found this person's front door and knocked loudly and woke them up. They spent the night sleeping on the couch and in the morning walked home to report the missing bag, cards and phone.

Does Sian have a problem? Is her drinking moderate or normal? If it weren't for the binge on that night out, would her level of consumption be OK? Do you think the night out was a one off or might it have happened at other times?

Eleanor's Story

Eleanor enjoyed a drink. And why not? She'd had a hard life and at seventy-seven she deserved a bit of relaxation. Her kids were all grown up with families of their own and they were all OK. She'd lived alone since her husband had left her ten years ago and as far as she was concerned it was good riddance. He had been a waste of space and drank far too much. Eleanor had a glass of beer every night and then a couple of large glasses of whiskey before bed. She'd wanted some pills to help her sleep, but her doctor had warned her not to mix pills with alcohol and she had preferred the whiskey. She hadn't gone to the doctor to talk about her sleep though. It was her digestion that had worried her, along with general aches and pains. The doctor had done a few tests which had proved negative and that was it. When she'd mentioned the alcohol, the doctor had said nothing about it — so Eleanor had assumed it was OK and carried on.

Is Eleanor's alcohol consumption putting her at risk? Was the doctor right not to mention anything?

Rob's Story

Rob doesn't get out of bed most days until around midday. He has no work and nothing he wants to do. Rob's first activity is to look in his pocket to see if he has any money. If he has, he walks round the corner to the local shop and buys a couple of cans of beer. If there are any cans in the fridge, though, he doesn't leave his flat at all on that day. He watches TV all afternoon and eats toast. At around 7.00pm he goes out to buy a takeaway and pick up another couple of cans. He might visit a friend for a while, but the evening is spent watching TV until the small hours. Most days are the same, except for those when he has no money. He sometimes gets a tin on credit but the shopkeeper only allows him to do this occasionally so there are days in which he has nothing to drink. On average, he drinks around twenty cans of beer each week.

Is Rob drinking safely? What role does alcohol play in his life?

Judy's Story

Judy works fulltime. Her job is very stressful and busy. She has two children at primary school who go to an after school club and are then picked up by a neighbour who looks after them until Judy gets home at 6.15pm. She gives the children their tea and hurries them off to bed as soon as she can. Then she starts to cook. She usually waits to open a bottle of wine until she starts cooking as she doesn't want the children to see her drinking. After dinner she settles down to watch TV. Her partner gets in around 9.00pm and by the end of the evening the bottle is three quarters empty. There's no point in wasting it, so they finish the bottle. At weekends, as they are busy with family and friends, they hardly drink at all, except, that is, for the nightcap just before bed — a finger of vodka or so!

How much do you think Judy is drinking each week? Is it possible to tell? Is Judy's consumption level safe?

It would be possible to give many more examples of the different roles alcohol plays in people's lives. And, of course, alcohol can also have a very positive function. It helps us celebrate and have fun. We use it to mark special occasions. It is sometimes part of religious ceremonies. It can help ease tense situations at social functions. It is a hobby and special interest for wine tasters and beer connoisseurs. It is a big part of the economy and generates taxes. And there some people who believe that in small quantities it is beneficial for health.

But what about you and the people you know? Is your drinking a problem?

How to Find Out If You Are Drinking Too Much

There are many different ways to assess whether you are at increased risk of harm from your drinking. The most common are questionnaires, and we will look at a few of them in this section. Be sure to note the wording carefully. The questionnaires help to determine if you are at increased risk of harm. They don't tell you whether you are experiencing harm, but whether you are at increased risk.

When you complete these questionnaires, you should try to answer them as honestly as you can. If you don't you are fooling no one but yourself.

Assessing Your Level of Risk

We will start with the AUDIT C (see figure 1). It is part of a bigger questionnaire called the Alcohol Use Disorders Identification Test (AUDIT) which was developed by the World Health Organisation and is considered to be the 'gold standard' for this type of questionnaire. The AUDIT C is an abbreviated version and is a standard screening test for increased risk and is widely used by doctors and other health service staff.

Add your scores up, and if you have a total of 5 or more this indicates increasing or higher risk of experiencing harms from drinking. (Sometimes the cut-off score is set at 4 not 5 — we are possibly being a bit lenient here).

If you scored 5 or more (or 4 or more) then you should probably be thinking seriously about the impact of your drinking levels. The remaining items of the AUDIT can help you do this (see figure 2).

If, when you add the scores of the two questionnaires together, you fall into the 0–7 range then you are at lower risk; if you scored 8–15 then you are at increasing risk; if you scored 16–19 you are at higher risk; and a score of 20 or more means you are possibly alcohol dependent.

	Scoring system					Your score
	0	**1**	**2**	**3**	**4**	
How often do you have a drink containing alcohol?	Never	Monthly or less	2–4 times per month	2–3 times per week	4+ times per week	
How many units of alcohol do you drink on a typical day when you are drinking?	1–2	3–4	5–6	7–9	10+	
How often have you had 6 or more units if female, or 8 or more if male, on a single occasion in the last year?	Never	Less than monthly	Monthly	Weekly	Daily or almost daily	
1 drink/unit = ½ pt beer or 1 glass of wine or 1 single measure of spirits.						

Figure 1   Calculating Your Intake (the AUDIT C)

Questions	Scoring system					Your score
	0	1	2	3	4	
How often during the last year have you found that you were not able to stop drinking once you had started?	Never	Less than monthly	Monthly	Weekly	Daily or almost daily	
How often during the last year have you failed to do what was normally expected from you because of your drinking?	Never	Less than monthly	Monthly	Weekly	Daily or almost daily	
How often during the last year have you needed an alcoholic drink in the morning to get yourself going after a heavy drinking session?	Never	Less than monthly	Monthly	Weekly	Daily or almost daily	
How often during the last year have you had a feeling of guilt or remorse after drinking?	Never	Less than monthly	Monthly	Weekly	Daily or almost daily	
How often during the last year have you been unable to remember what happened the night before because you had been drinking?	Never	Less than monthly	Monthly	Weekly	Daily or almost daily	
Have you or somebody else been injured as a result of your drinking?	No		Yes, but not in the last year		Yes, during the last year	
Has a relative or friend, doctor or other health worker been concerned about your drinking or suggested that you cut down?	No		Yes, but not in the last year		Yes, during the last year	

Figure 2   Assessing the Impact of Your Alcohol Consumption

Medical Considerations

At this point it is important to consider some potentially serious concerns. (We will only mention them briefly here and there will be more information in chapter 4.) Alcohol is a highly addictive drug and it is very important to take a responsible attitude towards it. If you have been drinking very regularly then you could be dependent and you should not make any changes without seeing your doctor and getting medical advice and supervision.

The Effects of Alcohol Withdrawal

Alcohol withdrawal symptoms can occur if you stop or reduce your drinking quickly. If you are dependent on alcohol, stopping quickly can be fatal. One way to know if you are dependent is if you have to have a drink to stop yourself shaking or craving alcohol. If you are dependent, you must see your doctor before trying to stop. However, most people can stop or reduce their drinking without medical supervision. In an emergency you should call an ambulance and go to hospital.

If you have withdrawal symptoms (or are worried about them) your doctor may be able to help you overcome them. Also, if you have health problems it is important to talk to your doctor as these problems may also be affected by your drinking.

Alcohol withdrawal symptoms may be mild, moderate or severe. Severe symptoms include a state of confusion and hallucinations, agitation, fever, fits and black-outs. Moderate symptoms include headaches, sweating, nausea, vomiting, loss of appetite, difficulty sleeping, paleness, rapid heart rate (palpitations), enlarged or dilated pupils, clammy skin, tremor of the hands and involuntary, abnormal movements of the eyelids. Mild symptoms include feeling jumpy, shaky, anxious or nervous, irritable or easily excited, emotional, depressed, tired, difficulty with thinking clearly, poor concentration, poor memory and bad dreams.

About 95% of heavy drinkers will experience some symptoms if they withdraw from alcohol. If the symptoms are mild they will usually disappear after a few days and do not require treatment. If you have any of the severe symptoms it is important that you see your doctor immediately.

In the UK further information can be obtained by phoning NHS Direct at any time: NHS Helpline 0800 22 44 88

If you live in Scotland you can also phone NHS24 08454 24 24 24.

In the United States, go to the Department of Health and Human Services website and search there for what you need: http://www.hhs.gov/safety/index.html

Some More Questionnaires That You May Find Useful

Alcohol Problems

This questionnaire is based on a research instrument called the Alcohol Problems Questionnaire. You don't have to score this; just answering the questions may give you cause to think.

During the last 6 months have you (answer yes or no)
1. Tended to drink more on your own than you used to?
2. Worried about meeting friends the day after a drinking session?
3. Had additional financial problems?
4. Sold or pawned belongings to buy alcohol?
5. Found yourself making excuses or lying about money?
6. Been in trouble with the police due to your drinking?
7. Lost your licence for drinking and driving?
8. Been physically sick after drinking?
9. Had diarrhoea after a drinking session?
10. Had any stomach pains after a drinking session?
11. Had any accidents after drinking?
12. Needed hospital treatment after drinking?
13. Lost any weight?
14. Been neglecting yourself physically?
15. Failed to wash for several days at a time?
16. Given up any hobbies you previously enjoyed due to your drinking?
17. Complained about your drinking?
18. Has someone tried to stop you from having a drink?
19. Has someone refused to talk to you because you have been drinking?
20. Has someone threatened to leave you because of your drinking?
21. Has someone had to put you to bed after you have been drinking?
22. Has someone refused to have sex with you because of your drinking?
23. Shouted at your spouse or partner after you had been drinking?
24. Injured your spouse or partner after you had been drinking?
25. Separated from your partner because of your drinking?
26. Been criticised by your children about your drinking?
27. Had rows with your children about your drinking?
28. Do your children tend to avoid you when you have been drinking?
29. Have your children tried to stop you from having a drink?
30. Found your work less interesting than you used to?
31. Been unable to arrive on time for work due to your drinking?
32. Missed a whole day at work after a drinking session?
33. Had a complaint at work about you being late or absent?
34. Had any formal warnings from your employers?
35. Been suspended or dismissed from work?

Figure 3   Alcohol Problems Questionnaire

You may have answered 'yes' to some of these questions and thought that the problem may not have been caused by alcohol directly. This doesn't matter as it is still a problem that you have to deal with.

The final questionnaire in this section is about dependency. You can be having problems caused by alcohol without being dependent, but it is still worth having a look at it. If you think that you may be dependent then the advice is to see your doctor.

Leeds Dependency Questionnaire

Here are questions about the importance of alcohol and/or other drugs in your life. Think about your drinking and other drug use in the last two weeks and answer each question by ticking the closest answer to how you see yourself.

	Never	Sometimes	Often	Nearly always
1. Do you find yourself thinking about when you will next be able to have another drink (drug)?	0	1	2	3
2. Is drinking (drug use) more important to you than anything else you might do during the day?	0	1	2	3
3. Do you feel your need for drink (the drug) is too strong to control?	0	1	2	3
4. Do you plan your days around getting alcohol (the drug) and drinking (using the drug)?	0	1	2	3
5. Do you drink (use the drug) in a particular way in order to increase the effect it gives you?	0	1	2	3
6. Do you drink (use the drug) morning, afternoon and evening?	0	1	2	3
7. Do you feel you have to carry on drinking (drug use) once you have started?	0	1	2	3
8. Is getting the effect you want more important than the particular drink (drug) you use?	0	1	2	3
9. Do you want to drink (use the drug) more when the effect starts to wear off?	0	1	2	3
10. Do you find it difficult to cope with life without alcohol (drugs)?	0	1	2	3

Figure 4   Leeds Dependency Questionnaire

There is no need to score this questionnaire (but if you want to then the information can be found at http://www.drugalcoholdetoxandrehab.co.uk/files/leeds-dependency-questionnaire.doc). The important thing is to think about your answers and what they may mean for you.

What About Other Effects of Drinking on Your Life?

A unit of alcohol contains lots of calories.

Gin, Vodka, Whisky, Sherry, Pernod:	about **60**
Martini, Wine, Liqueurs:	about **90**
Campari, Champagne:	about **110**
Beer, Cider, Lager:	about **180**
Special lager:	about **200 (1/2 pint)**

Figure 5   Calories in Alcohol

Alcohol is expensive.

Alcohol can interfere with the quality of sleep.

Alcohol can get in the way of a good sex life.

Alcohol can make you feel depressed.

Good News

As you work through this book, you will discover many more things about your drinking, but, so that we don't become too depressed, it is time to introduce a more positive note. There is a substantial amount of research evidence and personal experience that it is possible to change both drinking that is worrying (but not too serious) and levels of drinking that are more damaging. Even among people who are drinking very heavily and have serious problems, they may find that taking stock of their situation, and making decisions about what and how to change, can go a long way to sorting things out.

Change doesn't have to be an all-or-nothing decision. Stopping altogether may be right for some people, but most people are able to reduce the amount they drink, or change the way they drink, without stopping altogether.

CHAPTER 2

Assessing Your Own Drinking

This chapter is designed to help you undertake a detailed assessment of your own alcohol consumption and the impact it is having on how you are living your life. You need to know about your own drinking before making a decision about whether you want to make any changes. It is important to realise that the quality of the decision you make is very important. Good intentions are great, but you need to have thought things through carefully if you want to be able to stick to your resolutions.

Taking time to decide is helpful. Doing this properly can be hard work, but it is worth the investment. In what follows there will be quizzes and exercises to help the thinking process. You can do this in your head if you wish, but writing your answers down in a notebook can be extra helpful.

Making the right decision can take time, especially as it may not be immediately obvious what the right decision for you will be. Most people are ambivalent about change. They may not feel ready yet and they may not know what to do. There is no point in rushing ahead until the reasons for this ambivalence are properly understood. People drink for a variety of reasons and they may also feel that they experience some benefits from drinking. It is possible that you may not feel ready yet to give up the benefits, even though the rational part of your mind thinks that you should.

We can start with some very basic questions (see figure 6 below).

What did you come up with when you thought about these questions? If you feel sure that this is not the right time to start, or you are not currently concerned about your drinking, then you should be honest with yourself and come back to this book when you feel ready. This might be the case if someone else is pushing you to stop or reduce your drinking. But if you have any interest at all in finding out whether your drinking is OK for you then carry on with the book.

If you ticked 'yes' to any of the 'barriers to change' then you may find this chapter helpful as it will give you the information you may need. If you ticked 'yes' to either of the 'helpful' questions then you are on to a good start. And if you couldn't tick 'yes' to them then don't worry — there is a lot in the approach adopted in this book to help.

Is this a good time for you to be thinking about changing your drinking?
○ Yes
○ No

On a scale from 1 to 10 , how much does your current level of drinking concern you?

Not at All					Greatly Concerned				
1	2	3	4	5	6	7	8	9	10
○	○	○	○	○	○	○	○	○	○

How do you feel about learning how to change your drinking as of NOW? Do any of these barriers apply to you?

☐   I'm addicted to alcohol

☐   I'm too depressed to try

Some people are also aware of factors that can be helpful to them when they consider changing their drinking. Do any of the helpful factors below apply to you?

☐   I've done difficult things before. I can learn to do this

☐   I've lots of people around me who can help me through the change

Figure 6   Planning to Change Questionnaire

So here come some exercises to do. They are set out in a logical order so that the answers from one exercise feed into the next. But you don't have to do them in this order and could just select the ones that interest you if you prefer.

What Is Good and What Is Not So Good About My Drinking?

This exercise is designed to help you understand more about what you think of your drinking.

The exercise begins firstly by asking you what is positive about your drinking and then, when you have done that, you are asked about the negative side of your drinking.

What I Like and What I Think Is Good About My Drinking

Write a list of what you consider to be all the benefits of your drinking, that is, anything that you like about it or think of as being positive. Your list might include

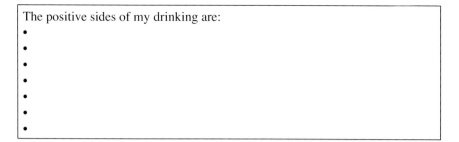

The positive sides of my drinking are:
-
-
-
-
-
-
-

Figure 7   Positive Sides of Drinking Worksheet

how it makes you feel, how it affects the way you relate to people and whether drinking sometimes seems useful. Most people have good reasons for doing what they do, and it is important to understand and be clear about your own reasons for drinking, and what benefits you get from it.

The Costs or Negative Sides of My Drinking

Write here a list of the other side of the coin — the costs or negative effects of your drinking. Include here anything you don't like about drinking or its consequences for you and others around you. This list might also include relationships and how alcohol makes you feel, as well as effects on health and well-being, work, money, or leisure activities. This should be as detailed and comprehensive as you can make it. It is important to think carefully and be fully honest with yourself about the not-so-good aspects of your drinking.

Remember this exercise is about your own drinking and not about the effects of alcohol in general.

The negative sides of my drinking are:
-
-
-
-
-
-
-

Figure 8   Negative Sides of Drinking Worksheet

The next task is to sort through this material and identify the personal significance of each of the items for you. A simple way to do this is by scoring them, from zero to three. For example, if a hangover doesn't really mean that much to you, just score it as 0. If, say, the effect on your finances is very important, then give a score of 3.

Here is a worked example — but you may have more items in your list:

The Positive Side of My Drinking		The Negative Side of My Drinking	
	Please score your responses for importance from 0 to 3		Please score your responses for importance from 0 to 3
I enjoy the taste of wine and beer	2	I am too tired to work properly the next day	3
It helps me to relax	3	I sometimes do embarrassing things which causes arguments	3
		I am overweight, drinking is the main reason	3

Figure 9   Positives and Negatives Summary Table

The final step is to see what it all adds up to.

If you ended up with many more benefits than costs, and the costs are not significant, there may be little reason to change your drinking.

If, however, the costs outweighed the benefits, there appears to be plenty of scope for thinking about change.

If there was no clear winner, and it is difficult to decide, perhaps this indicates the need for further thinking about your drinking.

> At this point you might want to be sure you have got it right by checking through the material for anything left out or not rated as importantly as it should be.

What Really Matters to Me?

This exercise is designed to help you decide how your drinking affects what is most important in your life.

The exercise starts with a technique called brainstorming. This is particularly useful when you need to break out of stale, established patterns of thinking, so that you can develop new ways of looking at things. It helps us to get clear about what we really think. There are three stages in this exercise (you will need a notebook). First, just answer the questions: What really matters to me? What are the most important things in my life?

Don't think about it too much — just write the things that first come into your head.

Don't judge what you write and don't edit. It doesn't matter if you change your mind — it's your first thoughts that are important.

We suggest you take no more than three to five minutes to do this.

> Think about the past, present and the future. What are your innermost hopes, dreams and fears? Include your values, ambitions and goals for yourself and also for other people. Put in anything at all that means a lot to you.

The second stage is to read through what you have written. Sort through it and pick out the most important things. Give this as much time as it needs, mull things over, and knock this list into shape. Turn your thoughts into a brief written statement that expresses the ideas that you have had.

The final stage is to consider carefully whether and how your current patterns of drinking harms anything that really matters to you and write this down in one or two sentences.

What have you discovered from this exercise? If you have concluded that drinking does not interfere with anything that really matters to you, then you might not have a good enough reason to change. If, however, you have discovered that drinking does interfere with what is important, then you do have reason to think more carefully about your drinking and consider the possibility of making changes. In fact, some people will have already decided at this stage that they have enough reason to change.

How Much Am I Drinking?

It is now time to get into some detail. What do you drink, how much do you drink, when do you drink, etc.? The rest of this chapter is devoted to giving you the information that can help you decide whether your drinking is OK, and if it isn't, why not. You can choose which exercises you want to do or you can choose to do all of them if you wish.

Before starting we have a few useful pointers:

- You already have some of this information. What we want to do is to bring this information into your thinking and decision-making in the simplest way possible.
- In these exercises you will be asked to remember specific things about your drinking. It is important to be as precise as possible when you are doing this and to say exactly what you mean.
- You will also be asked to give numbers to things. This approach may be new to you. It is important to realise that numbers never speak for themselves, they always need to be interpreted and we will help you do that.

Counting Drinks

Drinks vary in how much alcohol they contain, and a unit is a standardized measure of alcohol content. In the UK a unit is 8 g or 10 ml of alcohol; in the US it is 14 g or 18 ml; and in Ireland and many European countries it is

	Wine (abv)	Small glass (125 ml)	Medium glass (175 ml)	Large glass (250 ml)
	12%	1.5 units	2.1 units	3 units
	14%	1.75 units	2.5 units	3.5 units
	Beer (abv)	Half pint (248 ml)	Bottle (330 ml)	Pint (568 ml)
	4%	1.1 units	1.3 units	2.3 units
	5%	1.4 units	1.6 units	2.8 units
	Spirits (abv)	Single shot (small 25 ml)		Single shot (large 35 ml)
	40%	1 units		1.4 units

Figure 10   Measuring Units

10g or 12.7 ml. This makes comparison between countries difficult; but as long as you work in a consistent way and don't change systems then counting up units allows different drinks to be compared with each other. They can also be added up so that you can work out how much alcohol you are actually drinking in a given time period. It is the alcohol you drink which needs to be measured. It doesn't matter at all whether the alcohol was in a pint of beer, a glass of wine or a shot of spirits. And adding a mixer or a drop of water doesn't change the alcohol content, although it might mislead you into thinking you are drinking less alcohol. See the table above for some examples (using UK measurements).

Recording how much you actually drink in any given week can be a very helpful exercise. There are tools on the internet to help you do this. There is a drinking episode calculator at www.downyourdrink.org.uk, an alcohol unit calculator on the NHS choices website http://www.nhs.uk/Tools/Pages/Alcohol-unit-calculator. aspx and also on the BBC website at http://www.bbc.co.uk/newsbeat/12254668. In the US you can download an app for your phone from itunes. If you don't want to use an interactive tool then the chart below will do just as well (see figure 11).

Total up the amount of alcohol you consumed last week. It is important that you make a very definite effort to remember when you drank anything at all and exactly what you drank and how much; otherwise you will probably make a mistake and under-estimate.

All packaged drinks sold in the UK are required to provide information on the number of units they contain so you may be able to get the information you need from the labels on the bottle or can. You will still need to have a good awareness of units though, in order to calculate the alcohol content of drinks served in glasses.

How Much Alcohol?

To calculate the number of units in your drink without the unit calculator, you need to multiply the quantity (in ml) by the alcohol content (% abv), then divide

Day	Type of drink	Alcoholic strength (ABV)	Glass/ container size (see chart)	Number of drinks	Units	Total units for day
Sunday						
Monday						
Tuesday						
Wednesday						
Thursday						
Friday						
Saturday						

Figure 11   Charting Your Consumption Worksheet

by 1000. So, for a small single shot of vodka you would multiply 25 (ml) by 40 (% abv), then divide by 1000 which equals 1 unit.

When you have completed your diary for the last week add up the total number of units and see what you get. Is your result along the lines of what you had expected to get or are you surprised?

Blood Alcohol Level

People often worry about the amount of alcohol in their blood. So at this point we have provided you with some information to think about. 80 mg per cent means that there are 80 mg of actual alcohol in every 100 ml of blood. That is the legal limit for driving in the UK. In the US there are slightly different rules in each state, but overall the limit is similar to the UK limit. The amount allowed in Ireland and Australia is slightly lower at 50 mg. Although the legal limit for drinking is 80 mg per cent, you should not think that this means it is safe. Your reaction times, for example, will be slower and the chances of having an accident are twice those of when you have had nothing alcoholic to drink.
Remember !
• BAL measures the amount of alcohol, NOT the amount of beer or wine or whiskey or whatever.
• BAL measures the amount of alcohol in 100 ml of blood.

Blood Alcohol Level — Dilution
When you drink alcohol it is very quickly absorbed into all the body fluids including the bloodstream. The bloodstream takes the alcohol to the brain, which is where it affects you.

Small men are more affected than big men, because small men have less blood to dilute the alcohol in. Women are more affected than men because women have less body fluids to dilute the alcohol in. So, if a lot of different people each drank 2 units, they would have very different blood alcohol levels.

at B.A.L. of	Chances of having an accident
80 mg per cent	2 × risk when sober
150 mg per cent	10 × risk when sober
200 mg per cent	20 × risk when sober

Figure 12   Blood Alcohol Levels and Risk of Having an Accident

BAL mg per cent	What happens to you	
50	Merry, relaxed, cheerful	
80	Legal limit for driving	
100	Talkative, losing inhibitions	
150	Speech slurred, unsteady	
200	Staggering about, seeing double	
400	Oblivion, coma	
600	Death almost certain	

Figure 13   Blood Alcohol Levels and Behaviour

This table is a guide to what different blood alcohol levels mean.

DON'T FORGET: The legal limit for driving is a blood alcohol level of 80 mg per cent. But don't kid yourself that legal means safe.

You can use the table below to calculate approximate blood alcohol levels or there are calculators at www.downyourdrink.org.uk or at the NHS Choices website www.nhs.uk/chq

Alcohol Impairment Chart

Males

Approximate Blood Alcohol Percentage

Drinks*	Body Weight in Pounds								Effect on Person
	100	120	140	160	180	200	220	240	
0	.00	.00	.00	.00	.00	.00	.00	.00	Only Safe Driving Limit
1	.04	.03	.03	.02	.02	.02	.02	.02	Impairment Begins
2	.08	.06	.05	.05	.04	.04	.03	.03	Driving Skills Significantly Affected
3	.11	.09	.08	.07	.06	.06	.05	.05	
4	.15	.12	.11	.09	.08	.08	.07	.06	Legally Intoxicated
5	.19	.16	.13	.12	.11	.09	.09	.08	
6	.23	.19	.16	.14	.13	.11	.10	.09	
7	.26	.22	.19	.16	.15	.13	.12	.11	
8	.30	.25	.21	.19	.17	.15	.14	.13	Criminal Penalties in all States**
9	.34	.28	.24	.21	.19	.17	.15	.14	
10	.38	.31	.27	.23	.21	.19	.17	.16	

Females

Approximate Blood Alcohol Percentage

Drinks*	Body Weight in Pounds									Effect on Person
	90	100	120	140	160	180	200	220	240	
0	.00	.00	.00	.00	.00	.00	.00	.00	.00	Only Safe Driving Limit
1	.05	.05	.04	.03	.03	.03	.02	.02	.02	Impairment Begins
2	.10	.09	.08	.07	.06	.05	.05	.04	.04	Driving Skills Significantly Affected
3	.15	.14	.11	.11	.09	.08	.07	.06	.06	
4	.20	.18	.15	.13	.11	.10	.09	.08	.08	Legally Intoxicated
5	.25	.23	.19	.16	.14	.13	.11	.10	.09	
6	.30	.27	.23	.19	.17	.15	.14	.12	.11	
7	.35	.32	.27	.23	.20	.18	.16	.14	.13	
8	.40	.36	.30	.26	.23	.20	.18	.17	.15	Criminal Penalties in all States**
9	.45	.41	.34	.29	.26	.23	.20	.19	.17	
10	.51	.45	.38	.32	.28	.25	.23	.21	.19	

Subtract .01% for each 40 minutes of drinking.

* One drink is equal to 1¼ oz. of 80-proof liquor, 12 oz. of beer, or 4 oz. of table wine.

Figure 14   Alcohol Impairment Charts (Male and Female)

If you think you could drink a lot more alcohol without being affected than the calculation shows, then you have probably been drinking heavily for so long that you've just got used to it. It also means that you are no longer getting value for money for your drinks. You now have to buy a lot more than you did to get the same effect. And drinking a lot more harms you that much more.

Unfortunately, getting used to drink does not mean a lower BAL. Although you may not believe it, your legal BAL limit for driving is the same as for an inexperienced drinker.

Don't forget that when you are recovering from a hangover you may still be intoxicated but not realise it. And there is no way to speed up the rate at which alcohol leaves the body. Black coffee, cold showers, running on the spot make no difference.

One of the results of this slow burning process of alcohol in the body is that anyone whose BAL was 200 mg per cent at midnight will not be legal to drive to work at 8 o'clock the following morning.

Don't the police measure drunkenness in other ways? Yes. As well as blood, they can measure alcohol in urine and alcohol in breath. The legal limits for driving are:

In Blood	– 80 milligrams of alcohol in 100 ml of blood
In Urine	– 107 milligrams of alcohol in 100 ml of urine
In Breath	– 35 micrograms of alcohol in 100 ml of breath

Figure 15   Alcohol Limits for Driving

Safe Drinking Guidelines

How does your drinking compare with advice on sensible drinking? The UK Department of Health recommends that you shouldn't regularly drink more than:

3–4 units a day if you're a man, or

2–3 units a day if you're a woman.

Regularly means drinking every day or most days of the week. However, it's a good idea not to drink any alcohol at all on a few days each week. These guidelines are consistent with the ones adopted by the World Health Organisation. The WHO also states that you should not have more than 4 drinks on any one occasion.

Another way of thinking about drinking guidelines is to add up how much you drink each week (rather than calculating on a daily basis). If you do it this way, the UK guidance says the following:

1. Low-risk drinkers are those men who drink up to 21 units and women who drink up to 14 units per week.
2. Men who drink between 21–50 units and women who drink between 14–35 units are at medium risk, with your risk increasing the more you drink.
3. Men who drink above 50 units and women who drink above 35 units are at high risk.

> What is meant by *risk*?
>
> It's the likelihood that you have problems connected with the effect of alcohol on your health and well-being, either now or in the future

How Are My Drinking and the Consequences of My Drinking Changing Week to Week?

A good way to reflect on your drinking patterns is to keep a simple diary. The Unit Counter provided a snapshot of how to count one week's drinking. You can graph the amount you are drinking on a week-to-week basis. This is a good way to simply keep an eye on your overall drinking.

You can also monitor the patterns of your drinking in more detail if you keep a weekly record. There may be several aspects of your drinking that you may want to monitor — for example, drinking particular types of alcohol, or drinking with heavier drinkers, or in different places, or starting drinking early in the day or not finishing until late. These may all have different implications for both the amount you drink and the after-effects. It might be that you spot some interesting patterns to your drinking.

There is a simple example below. You can create a version for yourself that reflects the things you most want to monitor. There are also online versions and tools you can download to your computer or your phone at the NHS choices website: http://www.nhs.uk/tools/pages/nhsalcoholtracker.aspx (computer) http://www.nhs.uk/Tools/Pages/iphonedrinks.aspx (phone)

Another set of issues worth considering for a diary are the consequences of your drinking. Common examples are getting into trouble while drinking, being late or having a hangover at work, being moody or irritable, or simply being overly tired. To help assess which negative effects drinking may be having on your life, take some time to monitor what is going on. We call these drinking episodes. There are many other things you could choose to record, such as your reasons for beginning to drink each time, or the amount of money you spend. The more care you take in choosing what to monitor, the more helpful this exercise will be in gaining new learning about your drinking and its consequences.

Figure 16 is an example of a record of drinking consequences.

Looking Back at Your Drinking in the Past

Our behaviour changes for all sorts of reasons and it can be helpful to look back to earlier parts of our lives and reflect upon how and why these changes have occurred. The following exercise is designed to help you do this.

Select two or three different periods of time in the past when your drinking was significantly different to how it is now. Spend a little time recalling each of these periods in as much detail as possible. What were you drinking and how much? Who did you drink with, where did you drink, and what else was going in your life at the time? What were you doing and how were you feeling?

Day and time	Situation (e.g., who I was with, where I was)	What I was feeling and or thinking	What I drank	How many units I drank	What happened at the time	What happened next
Tuesday 9th October (lunchtime)	Talking on the phone to my Mum about her	Worried and upset	Wine	Most of the bottle (7 units)	Dozed off in the chair watching daytime TV	Couldn't be bothered to cook — ate toast
Wednesday 10th October	Dinner at home with Pete and Ingrid	Having fun, enjoying their company	Wine	3 glasses (3 units)	Enjoyed the meal and arranged to go their place next week	Slept well
Thursday 11th October (evening)	With Ian and Dave in pub	Angry because my team lost the match	Bottled lager, whiskey	4 bottles (5 units) 3 pub measures (3 units)	Got into an argument	Got to bed late, slept badly and couldn't concentrate properly at work next day

Figure 16   Sample Drinking Record

> Some people may initially find it difficult to identify times in the past when things were very different. It might seem like neither your drinking nor anything else in your life has changed for a long time. If this is your response then you could try changing the focus a little; you might ask yourself what are you like now compared to, say, 10 years ago. What differences are there between the way you were then and the you of today?

Take each one of these time periods in turn and compare it with your current drinking patterns and wider circumstances.

- What is similar and what is different?
- If it is helpful write down a few thoughts about the similarities and differences under the headings below:

                  Similarities   Differences

You might find the next part of the exercise straightforward or you might find it more complicated. Ask yourself how and why these changes occurred, and what implications they have had for your current patterns of drinking?

How Does My Drinking Compare to Other People's?

The more you drink the more your alcohol risk and problems are likely to increase. This is true for individuals and for the population as a whole. So you might find it helpful to compare your level of alcohol consumption with that of other people. Compare your consumption level with the average for your age and sex.

Average number of units drunk each week		
Age	Men	Women
16–24	21.5	14.1
25–44	18.7	8.4
45–64	17.5	6.7
65+	10.7	3.8
(This information is from the United Kingdom General Household Survey conducted in 2002)		

Figure 17   UK Average Weekly Levels of Consumption (2002)

In other countries the situation is different. In the US, for example, alcohol consumption is relatively low and there are many more people who either don't drink or drink very little compared to people in the UK. In France, Germany and other European countries, overall consumption of alcohol is higher than the UK, but fewer people drink heavily.

Heavy Binge Drinking Situations

Heavy or binge drinking can give rise to serious negative consequences and it has attracted a lot of media attention in recent times. Of course, there is nothing new about drinking more than you usually do and getting drunk. This has been happening for centuries! However, it does seem to be a particular problem in northern Europe and is a problem that is growing.

Binge drinking for men is defined as drinking more than 8 units of alcohol (about three pints of strong beer) on a single occasion. For women, it's drinking more than 6 units of alcohol, equivalent to two large glasses of wine, on a single occasion.

In this exercise the focus moves away from your relationship with alcohol in general to concerns about episodes of binge drinking. Your concern may be because of problems associated with heavy binge drinking, or it may be that you merely wish to take a closer look at what is going on in these situations.

In this exercise you might choose to focus upon a typical situation for you or on a recent episode. Focusing on a recent episode may help you to be more specific, or perhaps an unusual or unpleasant experience may have prompted you to do this exercise.

At the heart of this exercise are two simple questions:

1. What was happening before, during and after the drinking episode?
2. What was I thinking, feeling and doing during the episode?

You can create a table such as the one below to help you organise your thoughts:

Binge drinking can be quite common and may not be associated with regular heavy drinking. Remember the case study of Sian in chapter one. She drank regularly but the problem was the binge. The thoughts and feelings she would have had

	Before	During	After
What was happening	Had a row with Kirsty	Going over the argument in my mind	Sitting on my own
What I was thinking	I'm fed up with her	I don't care what she thinks	This is going nowhere
What I was feeling	Angry	Tense	Guilty
What I was doing	Watching TV	Drinking wine very quickly	Nothing

Figure 18   Sample Binge Drinking Record

would be different from the example in the table above. Maybe Sian's table would look something like this:

	Before	During	After
What was happening	I was going for a night out in a club with my friend	My friend kept buying drinks	In the toilet throwing up
What I was thinking	Meeting up with some guys I knew. Wondering what might happen.	Why not – I've had a few I may as well have another	Need to go home
What I was feeling	Nervous and apprehensive	Light headed and excited	Awful, embarrassed, upset
What I was doing	Dancing, talking, watching other people	Drinking very quickly	Crying

Figure 19   Sian's Binge Drinking Example

Doing this exercise for unusual heavy drinking episodes can also be very revealing. It can lead to new insights into how heavy drinking escalates. On the other hand, if there is a pattern that is recurring time after time, this may indicate something of concern. You can repeat this exercise as often as it seems useful to do so.

Putting It All Together and Coming to Some Conclusions

Now that you have done some or all of these exercises you are in a position to take stock and ask yourself: 'What do I really think about the downside to my drinking?'

Often people are aware of aspects of their drinking which are clearly not good and are certainly not wanted, and at the same time feel unsure about how much these really matter to them. There is a direct method for sorting this stuff out. Ask yourself the following question: 'What do I really think about the downside to my drinking?'

Categorise anything you don't like about your drinking in one of the following ways:

- Risks — these are anything that is a possible undesirable consequence of your drinking, but is not actually happening to you right now.
- Problems — these are anything that you don't like about your drinking that is currently happening. Defined in this way, it doesn't need to be a big deal to describe some aspects of your drinking as problems.
- Concerns — these are either risks or problems, but with a difference: They really do worry or trouble you, sometimes for reasons that are not at all clear. For example, you might keep turning over an issue in your mind.

Thinking It All Through and Getting Ready to Make Some Decisions

It can often seem that making sense of drinking is not at all easy to do. You can make up your mind one day and change it entirely the next. People can change their minds about their drinking because there are many things to consider and it really can be quite complicated. One way of describing it is to say that you are ambivalent about your relationship to alcohol. This means that there may be lots of ways in which drinking feels positive for you and other ways in which it seems that it is not. Ambivalence is perfectly normal. There are many things we do, like drinking, which it can be difficult to make up your mind about.

Another way of describing these dilemmas is to say that there are discrepancies between our behaviour, our values and personal goals — they don't fit together! Sometimes we just don't do what we think we should, and this is also nothing unusual.

If you feel that you are in a dilemma about whether or not to change your drinking here are some more ideas you might like to consider.

Touchy Subjects

Many of us have touchy subjects that produce a reaction. This can happen time and time again. These are usually things that other people say that are in some way connected to drinking. Usually they will occur with people who you know pretty well, but they can also arise in conversations with people you don't know as well. After the heat of a moment of annoyance or anger has passed then you may realise that there is an opportunity here to learn something about your reactions. These topics can then be subjected to a cool analysis of what they really say about your drinking.

You may not always get annoyed by these subjects. You may deal with them by becoming more quietly defensive, for example, steering the conversations away from the subject. The point here is first of all to spot what are these touchy subjects for you, and then to check them out to see whether thinking a little bit more about them is helpful.

Self-Directed Work and Setting Targets

Thinking through a complicated relationship with alcohol can take real time and effort. This book can provide support for this process, but it does not contain *the answer*; it is what you actually do that really matters.

Probably, having got to this stage, you have already done a fair amount of thinking work already. One very common and useful way to go on from here is to set targets or decision rules for yourself. Targets can relate to your overall drinking, for example, the total number of units you have in a week or a month. Or you can set a limit for the number of drinks you have on one evening.

Decision rules are about things you know that you want to do, or things you want to avoid doing. This could be things like not drinking certain types of drinks or not driving after drinking or other things you know you would regret afterwards. These are just examples and you will know best what is right for you.

If you do decide to set targets or rules, there are some things to remember. For example, a common mistake is to be over-ambitious at the start and misjudge what the target or rule should be. Keep it realistic!

So the preparation is over. By now you should have lots of information about your own pattern of drinking and have had the opportunity to think about it in some depth.

CHAPTER 3

How Does Change Happen?

Changing drinking habits might be quite a big deal for some people. Despite the best of intentions, it can be a hard thing to do and may have important knock-on effects for you, your lifestyle and the people around you. In the third part of this book we will take time to think about these things in detail. But at this point we are going to consider some important psychological factors involved in change that it might be helpful to know about in advance.

However, if you feel ready to change right now then you can skip this chapter and go straight to chapter 4, which is about medical information, or to chapter 5, which is about taking the plunge by making some detailed plans and putting them into action. But this chapter is designed to give you some more thinking time and, as you will see below, thinking things through properly is important. It is important because if the changes are going to work then careful planning is going to be helpful.

Alcohol researchers have developed numerous theories about how best to treat people with addictions or dependency; how best to help them to change. We will not look at all of the theories, but there are two particular psychological theories that are useful to know about at this stage. Although these were developed as theories about treatment, they can be adapted for people who don't need treatment, but are choosing to make changes on their own. The first is called the 'stages of change model,' which, as the name suggests, recognises that lasting change doesn't usually occur in one go and there are various stages that people often go through. The second theory is about motivation for change, which isn't straightforward. Even when people are keen to change and can understand all the reasons why change is a good idea, there is usually some ambivalence about actually making a change. There can be a thought in the back of the mind that they would really rather keep things at they are. This is normal and not laziness or a lack of will power, but the recognition of the reality that change is difficult. Individuals have many and varied reasons for drinking heavily in the first place and these reasons don't just go away. Change has costs as well as benefits.

In this chapter we will look at these two theories in a bit of detail. A lot has also been written about other psychological factors that influence drinking habits as well. We are focusing on these two models now because they are the most helpful to know about at this stage of the process. We will discuss other psychological models as we progress through the book. This does not mean that these other models are less important, but not everything can be covered at once and they will be introduced as we go along.

The Stages of Change

Some people do manage to summon up the will power and just stop. It may be after a significant event such as some bad news, perhaps a medical test has brought some worrying information; or it could be that you have made a new year's resolution to get fit. But this is relatively unusual. Mostly, people slowly come to terms with the idea of change and realise that to actually change they are going to have to put in some effort to make it happen. It can take a while to get used to the idea and thoughts often change before action.

Researchers have observed that, although people may be aware that they are drinking in a way that harms their health, they still have no real plans to do anything about it. They may have read newspaper articles, seen TV programmes about the hazards of regular drinking or discussed it with friends and family, but they have never seriously thought that they needed to change themselves. Change is for other people, not for them. This state is called 'pre-contemplation.' If they think about change at all then it is something for the future. Some people who are reading this book may be at this point. It could be that they are reading the book out of interest only or as something that may be useful for other people. As yet they don't think this book is about them personally. Let's go back to the case histories of the people we first met in chapter 1.

> As a young man Henry was drinking quite heavily and if he kept up that level of consumption he was running the risk of creating some health problems in later life. Yet he wasn't thinking about changing at all. To him this level of drinking was completely normal. At that point in his life Henry was in the pre-contemplation stage.

> It is a similar story with Sian. She was drinking regularly but there is no thought of change. Not until that fateful night out, when she put herself in a risky situation. Rob and Judy were also not contemplating change. But what about Eleanor? Her situation was a little bit different. Eleanor was wondering if her alcohol consumption was OK, and, as we saw, her doctor may have missed an opportunity to help her tackle this issue.

The crucial move to make is from pre-contemplation to contemplation. Contemplation is important. During contemplation, a person may become aware of the pros and cons of their drinking, the impact it is having on their lives and they might make some plans to change. Contemplation is an active process. It might involve some detailed thinking and planning. The work of chapter 2 in this book was about contemplation. Contemplation is about getting to grips with your own personal alcohol story and making some decisions about the role you want alcohol to play in your life.

Sometimes contemplation can take a long time, but hopefully it then leads on to preparation. We will help you with this in chapter 5. There is a lot to think about and the more detailed the planning the better. That is, as long as planning doesn't become a substitute for change. There is always the risk of that. Thinking about how you are going to change in the future can be a hell of a lot easier than actually doing it. And there can be some comfort in this kind of thinking. People can delude themselves that they are doing the right thing by going over and over in their minds how bad drinking is, what they plan to do about it and how great life will be when they have made the changes. This is daydreaming and not real contemplation or preparation. They may even do it with a glass in their hands! It is one of the many traps to avoid on this journey.

> Henry fell into this trap. He knew that when things had got bad between him and his partner, and he had home stress and work stress, that he was drinking too much. As a young man he hadn't thought about his consumption level at all, but he knew not to drink too much before an important meeting at work and that was about as far as his thinking went. When he was spending a lot of time and money on alcohol he had realised that alcohol was major prop in his life. He thought about going to the gym, improving his diet and cutting down the booze. He'd mentioned this to one or two people at work and they had also thought that it was a good idea. It made him feel better to talk about how he was going to 'get a grip.' But nothing changed and he carried on drinking.

The next step in the change cycle is action. It might appear that this is the most important phase but actually it often isn't. The planning is really important and once you have decided to make a change and what change to make then you just have to actually do it — put the plan into action. If it's a good plan and reasonable then the plan will work! Sometimes the action phase is the quickest of them all. Of course, you may have to do it again but that is another story and we will come back to it.

> After Sian's disastrous night out she got really scared. She decided that she did not want to put herself in a similar situation again, so she had a good long chat with her friend. Her friend hadn't initially seen what the problem was, but Sian said that was just bravado and they needed to sort it. They worked out together that the preloading was the problem along with the cheap drinks in the early part of the evening. They planned to miss out the cider and not arrive at the club until later in the evening. Sian confessed to her friend that the reason she drank so much was because she was nervous about meeting new men. Her friend said that she sometimes felt the same way, and they agreed to support each other when they next went out and not to split up or go off on their own. They would also plan to drink water as well as alcohol when they were dancing.

Sticking to the plan is the hard bit. This is the maintenance phase and the third part of this book is devoted to the topic. While action may happen quickly, maintenance has to be long because it is about living with the changes you have made and keeping them going. Sometimes maintenance isn't long at all because the person cannot stick to the changes and they go back to the old pattern. This is called relapse. The key thing here is to not drop out of the circle altogether. If you do relapse then it is time to go back to the drawing board and do some more planning. One of the key features of the stages of change model is that the phases are arranged in a circle (see diagram). Relapsing isn't necessarily a problem, and as long as you stay within the cycle of change, learn from experience and go back to the action stage then not much is lost. Some people go round the circle many times before they are successful. If, however, you lose hope, think change is not possible and go back to pre-contemplation, then there is a problem and you have left the circle.

The other way of leaving the circle is when the maintenance of the changes has become so well engrained that your new habits have become really well established. This is called the stable phase and is where we all hope to be.

The stages of change model is not without controversy. There is a point of view that these stages don't really exist at all and don't always occur in this order. This is probably correct and there is certainly nothing compulsory about any of the stages! However, the model does seem to hold true for many people, and the important lessons of thinking before you act, being patient and learning that you may need to try many times before the changes stick are still important and useful.

The cycle of change model was originally developed to explain how people stop smoking. It was later extended to drinking problems and other types of behaviour. With smoking the goal is fairly straightforward to describe: to stop, give up, halt! With drinking the task is a bit more complicated. For some people abstinence or going teetotal is a perfectly sensible goal. But it doesn't suit everyone and some people will opt to reduce their consumption or adopt what is called 'controlled drinking.' This means that it is not always clear which stage someone is in. If your

The process of change

Figure 20   The Cycle of Change

plan allows you to have an occasional drink, or even more than the occasional drink, then, if you have a little bit more than you planned, should this be considered a relapse or is it OK and part of the maintenance stage? We will come back to this later in the book.

Motivation

In chapter 2 we introduced the idea that the quality of the decision to change is crucial. The decision to change something as major as your drinking behaviour is rarely done successfully on a whim. And it is not something that can be forced on you. If change is to be successful then it must flow from a desire to change and, importantly, a thorough understanding of what you have to gain and to lose, what fits best with your lifestyle and your values, and the effects that your drinking has on the people around you.

The experience of trying to force someone to do something they don't want to do can be very unpleasant. And it rarely works. In fact, what happens when pressure is applied is that people will often react against the pressure and be even less likely to change. It can harden opinions. The same is true if you try to frighten someone into changing. Showing people pictures of rotting livers, car crashes caused by drunken drivers or babies damaged by foetal alcohol syndrome rarely has the desired effect. People have a myriad of ways to deflect the information. They can ignore it, deny it or find a way of saying that it doesn't apply to them. In the next chapter we will be giving you some health related information, but not to try and frighten you into change.

The understanding of motivation to change that underpins this book is adapted from an approach to treatment called motivational interviewing. With this approach a counsellor will spend time with a client one to one. During the conversation they will talk about someone's drinking from a variety of angles. The counsellor asks open ended questions to try to learn more about what a person's attitude towards alcohol is so that they can learn to see things from the client's point of view. And they will try to ask about the level of consumption in a non-threatening way. They will make lists of the pros and cons of change, the implications of keeping things as they are and any downside or costs there may be to changing. The decision to change or stay the same belongs to the client and there is no attempt to persuade or coerce them. The counsellor will work towards helping the client to develop a plan based on all this information that is right for the client and one that the client is happy with. During the course of these conversations the client may show resistance. This is when the client experiences a conflict between the problem that they have and a solution that the counsellor (or doctor, family member or friend) is suggesting. The client may express this by indicating that they do not want to make a change or be worried or unhappy about the idea. The task of the counsellor is to 'ride' with this resistance. It is normal and natural for someone to be ambivalent; the counsellor recognises this and accepts it. They do not confront it head on, but leave the client to make the choices. The case study of Judy in chapter 1 illustrates this situation quite well.

Judy is reasonably happy with her drinking. In the language of the stages of change, she is at the stage of pre-contemplation. She is probably drinking more than double the recommended limits for a woman and if she continues this way she is likely to be putting her health at risk. But at the moment she is not aware of this. Now imagine that she goes to see her doctor for something routine and the doctor does a quick health check while she is there. The doctor checks on weight, blood pressure etc., and then asks some questions about smoking, exercise and drinking. All is fine until she mentions the drinking. At this point the doctor has some choices to make. He or she could ignore the issue (and many doctors do), they could warn Judy that this level of drinking may be detrimental to her health, they could lecture her about the awful things that might happen to her if she carries on drinking, they could give her a diary to record how much she drinks each day, or they could simply tell her to stop drinking so much. The doctor chose to ask her to think about her drinking and said that a note would be made to ask her about it again at her next check up. Judy's immediate reaction was to feel surprised and a bit affronted. She hadn't gone to the doctor to talk about drinking and wasn't ready to even think about it, let alone do anything about it. When she got home she began to feel quite annoyed about the doctor's comments and didn't say anything about it to her partner. Later in the evening, however, after a couple of drinks, she mentioned to her partner that she might be drinking a little too much and perhaps they could save some money by cutting down.

Other Psychological Ideas

Psychological models of change are not restricted to the stages of change and motivational interviewing approaches. In fact, there is a whole industry of psychological research into addictions and dependency that can be applied. Some models are more relevant than others and quite a few make an appearance at points in this book. We will briefly review some of them now as they might provoke some useful thoughts or insights.

We will start with twelve step programmes, made famous by organisations such as Alcoholics Anonymous (AA). These programmes are great for some people, but there are also some people who don't find them helpful at all. They are aimed primarily at people who feel they are addicted to a substance or behaviour and the first step is always for the person to accept that they have a problem. This can be the most difficult step of all. The programme is a group programme and can provide a tremendous amount of support, particularly when an individual is assigned a mentor to guide and support them. A key component of the approach is that the goal is abstinence. Members of AA see themselves as addicts and that remaining alcohol free is a lifelong task. Although AA doesn't suit everyone, it is difficult to think of an organisation that has done more to support and help people addicted to alcohol. The approach in this book doesn't follow the twelve step approach; but if you are someone who feels that they have an addiction to alcohol then you could check them out (as well as seeing your GP to ensure that the physical side of addiction is taken care of safely).

Psychologists have researched into the effects alcohol has on a person and have developed some useful insights. One of these is that some of the reasons people enjoy alcohol contribute to the harms it creates. Alcohol affects decision making, judgment and can make you lose your inhibitions once you have started drinking, so then it can be difficult to stop drinking. This is not exactly rocket science, but sometimes the obvious is worth pointing out! Alcohol is also a depressant so drinking can make you miserable (especially if you are feeling down anyway).

Drinking alcohol can be habit forming. Not just because we can become dependent on the effects of alcohol, but also because we sometimes continue drinking due to learned behaviour. Drinking habits can develop over time and can then be difficult to change. We saw this in the case of Henry who saw his parents drink regularly (modelling) and he also learned to use alcohol to help him cope with the ups and downs of his emotional life. Sian had learned to use alcohol to cope with anxiety and problems with self confidence. Judy had learned that alcohol helped her to feel more relaxed and used it as a reward at the end of a busy day. This understanding of the behavioural aspect of drinking is very important and has led to many very practical approaches to helping people resolve drinking problems. It has proven to be just as effective as motivational interviewing in treatment and the third part of this book is largely based on this approach. The techniques and strategies that have developed out of this behavioural research are vital ingredients in relapse prevention.

An additional element to the role of learned behaviour is 'cognition.' Cognition is about the way we make sense of things or interpret what happens. Taken together behavioural approaches and cognitive approaches are called cognitive behaviour therapy (CBT). One research finding concerning the role of cognition in drinking alcohol is a bit surprising. The experience of feeling inebriated is not entirely due to the chemical effects of alcohol on the brain. It is also influenced by a person's expectation of what will happen when they drink. If you expect that alcohol will make you feel relaxed, happy and more sociable then it probably will. While it is not all 'in the mind,' some of it is!

Drinking often takes place in a social context. While some people drink alone, there are many others who drink with friends, neighbours, work colleagues, family, sports team members and casual acquaintances. Changing drinking may also mean that you will be changing your relationship with all these people as well. Social behaviour and network therapy (SBNT) was developed to help people build new social networks to help overcome this problem. In a large research study in the UK, it worked just as well as approaches based on motivational interviewing. There is plenty from this approach to be found in the chapters that follow as well.

CHAPTER 4

Alcohol and You: What Are You at Risk of?

In chapter 1 you were invited to take a short test (the AUDIT C). If you scored 5 or more you were told that you were at increased risk of experiencing harms related to your use of alcohol. But we didn't tell you what kinds of harm you were at risk of. The list of possible harms is quite long and we don't want to frighten you; but, on the other hand, we do think you have a right to the information. If you are interested in learning more then read on. If not, then skip to the next chapter.

General Health

If you have not been drinking too much for too long then you may not have done yourself any permanent harm. At least not yet! But continued drinking does damage different parts of the body — slowly but surely.

The active ingredient in wine, beer and spirits is ethyl alcohol (ethanol). This is an intoxicating substance that arises naturally in certain processes that involve the fermentation of carbohydrates. Alcoholic drinks have lots of calories and some heavy drinkers put on weight; but that is not true of all heavy drinkers as some people become underweight — it is a bit of a confusing picture. Regular drinkers may also not eat regularly or have a balanced diet. Another effect that alcohol has is to interfere with the way the body controls the amount of sugar in the bloodstream. In some cases this can lead to diabetes and even brain damage.

But want about health benefits? There has been quite a lot of discussion in the media about whether a moderate amount of alcohol is actually good for you. Is a glass of red wine good for the heart, for example? This question is about moderate drinking and the chances are that the people who are reading this book are not drinking moderately. Moderate drinking for women would be no more than one glass of wine a day and for men no more than two glasses per day. These are generalizations and the actual effects of alcohol on the body depend quite a bit on your age, health, weight, general health, diet, lifestyle and activity levels. And, of course, there are other considerations that it is important to think about: are you taking medication, do you have a health problem and are you pregnant or thinking of becoming pregnant? If any of these are true for you then you should be questioning whether any alcohol is okay. The information that follows is where the science is in 2012. It could change, but be sure that you don't use any of this information to justify drinking.

So, back to the red wine: There is quite a bit of evidence that drinkers have a lower rate of heart disease than non drinkers. But that doesn't necessarily mean that drinking alcohol is protective, or if it is protective how much alcohol is actually required to achieve any advantage that there may be. It has been suggested, for example, that a glass of red wine each day may have a beneficial effect on the coronary system. Could it be that it is the antioxidants present in red wine that are good for the heart? The evidence for this suggestion is tenuous indeed. It comes from laboratory studies on mice and not much is known about the actual implications for humans. The chemical in question is found in the skin of the grapes used to produce red wine not in the alcohol. So if you want any possible benefits there might be then you may as well drink red grape juice. And if you choose this option then you won't have the problem of the alcohol you have drunk undoing any good work by destroying vitamins (see below). However, there is also another medical viewpoint that it is actually the alcohol in the wine that is beneficial provided it is no more than one unit a day. This debate about the possible value of drinking red wine continues and it can't be resolved here. However, what is clear is that drinking a lot is likely to be harmful.

A word of warning: It is quite common for people to read medical textbooks and start to think that they are suffering from all the diseases mentioned in the book. This happens to medical students as well as the general public. Drinking can cause problems and it can also disguise them. Don't make the mistake of assuming you are able to judge if something is wrong with you. A little knowledge can be a dangerous thing and if you are at all worried then make sure you go and see your doctor. And if you are going to look things up on the internet the same rules apply.

What Happens to the Liver?

Alcohol is absorbed by the body extremely quickly. It is not like most of the things we normally eat or drink which requires time for digestion. The body uses alcohol before most other nutrients, and alcohol can reach the brain within about one minute. Most people who have had a drink know this already as they rapidly feel the effects. Alcohol is also absorbed quickly by the intestines and enters the bloodstream rapidly. From there it goes on to the liver, which sets to work cleaning up the blood. The liver is the only organ in the body that can do this efficiently. Only about 10% of the alcohol we drink is expelled in the breath and urine.

The problem for the liver is that its regular work is to deal with fatty acids. But when there is alcohol in the blood stream, the liver prioritizes the alcohol and the fatty acids build up. If someone drinks regularly, the liver cell structure may change permanently and the liver stops working properly, which can lead to nutritional problems. The liver can become inflamed and the liver can be scarred (cirrhosis). An enlarged liver is often a diagnostic sign that is something is wrong. Although these problems don't usually happen after moderate drinking, even a single heavy night could have some damaging effects.

There are lots of calories in alcohol, but there are very few nutrients and none in pure alcohol at all. From this point of view it is quite like eating spoonfuls of sugar — it provides empty calories. Drinking a lot may mean you put on weight. And the more calories you get from alcohol the less you may feel like eating proper food. Alcohol also destroys some of the goodness that is normally present in healthy food. In particular, you lose vitamin C and many types of vitamin B. This is not good for you and people who drink heavily for a long time can end up with serious nutritional problems. The depletion of vitamin B can have serious effects on the brain causing severe memory loss. In fact the nutritional problems produced by hazardous drinking can damage every organ in the body.

The list of possible diseases from excessive alcohol consumption is very long and makes depressing reading. You don't have to read them, but here they are: arthritis (especially gout), cancer (most of the major organs), foetal alcohol syndrome (effects on the unborn), heart disease, hyperglycaemia (too much sugar in the blood), hypoglycaemia (lower blood sugar in the blood — especially if you have diabetes), kidney disease, liver disease, malnutrition, nervous disorders, obesity, anxiety, traffic accidents, industrial accidents, depression and insomnia. Usually the worst of these only happens when people have been drinking heavily for a long time. But some people can be unlucky, especially if they also have other health problems, and they get ill quickly.

Alcohol and the Brain and Nervous System

Most people know that drinking too much alcohol affects concentration, memory, reaction time, judgment, etc., but what about long-term consequences? The more you drink the bigger the effects, and if you drink a lot on an empty stomach then you can black out and have amnesia.

A history of heavy drinking can lead to peripheral neuropathy. This is nerve damage that can affect one nerve or a whole group of nerves causing pain, numbness, muscle problems, organ damage, sexual problems, bladder problems, excessive sweating — a long list. It can also lead to brain shrinkage that can be seen on brain (CT) scans. Heavy drinking over a long period can lead to a shortage of thiamine, which causes serious memory problems and confusion (Wernicke and Korsakoff Syndromes).

We saw above that long term heavy drinking can result in liver problems. The consequence of liver problems is that then bad stuff gets into the brain and can cause brain damage (hepatic encephalopathy). The symptoms can be changes in sleep patterns, mood, and personality; anxiety and depression; shortened attention span and problems with coordination.

It is not all entirely doom and gloom. If people stop drinking then there can be improvement in symptoms and there are some treatments. But, overall, the effects of heavy long-term drinking on the brain and nervous system are, unfortunately, dire.

Alcohol and Age

Let's start at the beginning — with babies. The advice given to women is to be very careful about their drinking when they are pregnant or planning to become pregnant. This is very sensible advice indeed. Some research has suggested that there may be no safe level of drinking during pregnancy, but, clearly, the higher the level of consumption the greater the possible impact on the unborn child. We don't yet know whether moderate drinking causes problems and at what level of consumption drinking causes serious harms. There is probably quite a bit of variation between people. And men need to be aware as well! Alcohol may affect the health and viability of the sperm.

The term *foetal alcohol syndrome* was coined over 30 years ago to describe the role alcohol consumption has on birth defects. The sad list of very serious harms includes facial abnormalities, growth problems and cognitive impairment.

Babies turn into children and there is much that can be said (and often is) about whether children should be allowed to drink any alcohol at all. Most families will have discussed this at some time and attitudes differ. The debate will not be resolved here, but we will suggest some things to think about. However, we need to start with the legal situation. In most countries there are laws about what is legal and what is not. This is the situation in the UK.

It is against the law:[1]

- to be drunk in charge of a child under seven in a public place or on licensed premises
- to sell alcohol to someone under 18, anywhere
- for an adult to buy or attempt to buy alcohol on behalf of someone under 18
- for someone under 18 to buy alcohol, attempt to buy alcohol or to be sold alcohol in any circumstances (unless acting at the request of the police or a weights and measures inspector)
- for someone under 18 to drink alcohol in licensed premises, with one exception: 16 and 17 year olds accompanied by an adult can drink but not buy beer, wine and cider with a table meal
- for an adult to buy alcohol for a person under 18 for consumption on licensed premises, except as above

It is not illegal for a person under 18 to drink alcohol at home or at a friend's house. Parents can choose to give young people some of their own alcohol when at home. But that doesn't mean that it is a good idea. However, many adults want to introduce their children to alcohol under controlled circumstances or simply like sharing it (remember the case study of Henry in chapter 1). And there are different customs in different countries and cultures.

Here is an interesting observation to ponder: Adult alcoholics are more likely to have parents who were either teetotal themselves or were alcoholics. The current medical advice is that children should not drink alcohol at all, but there are many doctors who do not agree with this.

---

[1]http://www.direct.gov.uk/en/Parents/Yourchildshealthandsafety/WorriedAbout/ DG_10026211

But what about the possible harms? Alcohol affects children more quickly than adults (because of their size), and a visit to any accident-and-emergency department will confirm that sometimes children can become very ill indeed through alcohol. And the damage they suffer may have long term effects which might not be seen until they are older. Also, drinking by adolescents can increase risk taking (which they do anyway) and interfere with their judgment. So an otherwise sensible 16-year-old might do some very stupid things when drunk — including drug taking, risky sex, becoming aggressive and committing crimes.

We can skip now to older people. When does old age start? And is age important when thinking about alcohol consumption? It is interesting that many people say that they started drinking more after they had retired. So perhaps it is a life stage thing rather than age itself. Also, retired people may drink at home and drink alone. You don't need to go out to get alcohol — it can arrive with the weekly supermarket shopping delivered direct to the door.

Alcohol can make the ordinary problems of aging worse. If you are frail then you may have more falls and that can lead to more fractures; diabetes and high blood pressure can get worse; and if you are depressed then you are likely to feel worse rather than better. And alcohol can play havoc with sleep (see section on sleep below). Older people take more medicines than younger people and alcohol can sometimes stop the medicine working properly or make you ill. Regular drinking can also hide illnesses. Someone who is drinking may not notice pains or symptoms so they don't go to the doctor to get themselves checked out. In this way, serious illnesses such as heart disease may get missed.

Older people can be affected by alcohol more quickly than younger people. Their blood alcohol concentration levels increase more rapidly and also they tolerate alcohol less well. This means that someone may carry on drinking at the same level as they did when they were younger, but they start to experience harmful effects that they previously didn't have. Drinking can speed up the effects of aging on the brain. This means that memory, coordination and concentration can get a lot worse.

Alcohol and Sleep

Many people say they use alcohol to help them sleep. They enjoy a nightcap. But they might be less enthusiastic about this if they understood more about the way alcohol actually affects sleep.

It is certainly true that alcohol can help someone drop off to sleep — at least at first. But if used regularly for this purpose the effects may wear off. And the quality of sleep is not good. During the first half of the night the sleeper may sleep lightly and have fewer periods of the kind of sleep that is associated with dreaming. And during the rest of the night they don't catch up. Add to this the effects of having to visit the toilet several times and the result is poor quality sleep that isn't refreshing. The impact of this can be felt during the next day. People who use alcohol to get themselves off to sleep can feel tired most of the time. And if combined with medication (of whatever type) sleep can be very disrupted and possibly dangerous.

Are Genetic Factors Important?

A lot of people will want to know if some of us are more susceptible to have alcohol related problems because of our genes. A related question is whether some people have an inherited vulnerability to suffer organ damage through alcohol consumption. Whilst it seems unlikely that there is a single gene that can account for alcohol dependency, it may be that combinations of genes play a role. This role may not be direct; it could be that genetic factors contribute to vulnerability by influencing someone's temperament and that is combined with things that happen to us as we develop and our individual circumstances. The current consensus is the environmental factors are more important than genetic ones.

The research conducted so far tends to be about alcoholics rather than people who are not dependent but who drink more than they want to. So the observation that alcoholism runs in families, or that the children of alcoholics are four times more likely to become alcoholic than other children, is not that helpful, or relevant. Whilst it is possible that there is a genetic component, there is some evidence that the genetic contribution is to develop a general vulnerability to anxiety or other common problems, and not specific to alcohol.

Summing Up

In chapter 2 there was an opportunity to list all the down sides of your drinking. Having read through this chapter you may want to add a few more items to your list. Alcohol can affect many different parts of the body and the way the body works. This chapter isn't exhaustive and there may be others that could be added. In fact, it is difficult to think of an organ or system in the body that is not affected by drink. But the body often recovers when drinking is brought back to safer levels. If you are drinking at a level where you are worried that it may be making you ill then it is time to go and see your doctor. But if you want to make some changes then the place to start is chapter 5. And the time to start is now.

PART 2

Making the Change

CHAPTER 5

What Change is Right for Me?

Enough of theory! The next step is to make some decisions about what changes are right for you at the moment. There are some traps to avoid here. For example, you may be tempted to be a bit overdramatic. You might decide, for example, that you will stop drinking altogether from this moment. Or you might be a bit timid, saying I will only change a little bit and will start next week. The main things to remember are to make a well informed balanced choice and that the aim is to reduce any harm that you may be inflicting on yourself or on others.

Strategies and Approaches

There are three main ways of reducing the risk from your drinking:

1. Drinking less: cutting down the overall amount of absolute alcohol you are drinking will reduce your risk of harm.
2. Altering your pattern: if you know that particular aspects of your drinking have been problematic you could specifically target these for change, e.g. drinking spirits, going on a bender, drinking heavily after work, etc.
3. Giving up altogether: this might be a good idea if you have previously tried and repeatedly failed to achieve either of the previous two types of goals, or it might just suit you better anyway.

Whichever you decide is right for you, do keep in mind that sudden reductions in alcohol may be dangerous. So if you are in the habit of drinking regularly and are concerned that you might be dependent on alcohol, then it is absolutely vital that you seek medical advice before you do anything suddenly. This also true if you have any health problems.

You can't expect change to be straightforward. It may be useful to look back at chapter 2 and read again what you said your main obstacles to change might be. You will need to keep these in mind as you set your goals. Thinking about the case studies in chapter 1 can also suggest some barriers that could apply to you.

Henry

Imagine that Henry decided to change his drinking. There are some hefty obstacles that he will need to deal with. He has been drinking a long time (since childhood really) so he has definitely got the drinking habit. He uses alcohol to deal with emotional problems and may not have the skills to deal with his problems in any other way. He only has the vaguest idea of how much he actually drinks and doesn't really think that heavy drinking is much of a problem. He has got a lot of serious thinking and planning to do before he can really settle on a goal that he has much chance of achieving. This doesn't mean he can't, but it does mean that it may be very hard work.

What about the others?

Sian

Sian had a big fright and she is certainly determined not to put herself at risk again. But changing her drinking may mean that she won't go out as much, won't see her friends and will be nervous about talking to people she doesn't know, especially guys. This is quite a lot to lose and the chances are that she will find herself in a similar situation again if she is not careful. She certainly wants to cut out the pre-loading — but can she?

Eleanor

Eleanor is very worried that without a drink she won't be able to sleep. And there is no-one encouraging her to cut out the night time drink and, in fact, there is no-one actually noticing that she is drinking at all!

Rob

Rob has a lot to gain from cutting down his consumption. A plan to reduce might work for him, but he is also going to need to make some other fairly radical changes in his life.

Judy

Judy has lost track of how much alcohol she puts away each week. She can afford it and her partner hasn't got a problem with how much she drinks. If she were to cut down then her partner might be a bit surprised and may find it difficult to adjust to. He drinks as well and it is possible that any reduction by Judy might seem to imply that he should drink less as well.

Making the Decision

Have you thought of doing an experiment? Sometimes we are not sure whether changing something might be very difficult to do or reasonably easy. You could try doing an experiment to find out!

For example, if going home from the pub earlier than usual (say at 10 o'clock on a Wednesday night) is a possible change, you may be a little worried about how it will go down with your friends in the pub. You could just try it out to see what happens. Plan exactly what you want to do, then do it, and see how it goes. Make sure that your 'experiment' is as close as possible to the real situation. So, in this example, don't use a 'one-off' reason that you can't use week after week. Then you'll know what level of difficulty is actually involved.

Trying out possible changes in this way can be a useful method for working out what are the real obstacles to change and which change is best for you. Here are some suggestions about how to do the experiment:

1. Define the situation as closely as possible:
   Example — I will drink only 2 glasses of wine this evening.
2. What do you think might happen?
   Example — I'll get 'the taste' and not be able to do what I planned, which was to drink water between glasses of alcohol and I will end up drinking a whole bottle.
3. What will the experiment be?
   Example — I'll set the table with 2 glasses, one for water and one for wine. I'll keep a jug of water on the table and put the bottle of wine in the cupboard so I have to fetch it each time I want to fill my glass; and I will make sure I put the bottle back in the cupboard after filling it. I will count how many glasses of wine I have by making sure that I don't fill my glass again until it is empty, and I will note down in a notebook each time I empty the glass.
4. How will I know how well the experiment has gone?
   Example — I'll be able to see how much I have drunk.
5. What are the results of the experiment?
   Example — I drank 3 glasses rather than 2 (not bad for a first go).

Here is a form to fill in yourself and try:

Experiment Worksheet
1. Define the situation as closely as possible
2. What do you think might happen?
3. What the experiment will be?
4. How will I know how well the experiment has gone?
5. What are the results of the experiment?

Figure 21   Experiment Worksheet

The Decision and the Plan

Now you specify the exact nature of your decision and write it out so that it is clear what you need to do. There is nothing quite like writing things down to clarify exactly what your task is and making a commitment to carrying it through. You need to remember your original intention, which is to find a way of reducing the harm that alcohol may be causing.

In what follows there are a series of questions for you to address. Try to answer every one of these questions and add some more of your own if they occur to you and seem useful.

Most of this material is stuff you will already have given some thought to. Perhaps the newest heading is the one on how other people can help, and you might like to give this one some additional time. It is not a good idea to leave this one blank. There is research that shows that getting other people to support your decision can be very useful indeed.

Start answering these questions soon and be prepared to review what you have put early and often! It is very unlikely that you will be satisfied with your answers straight away. It is part of a process and going back over things once or twice can be very helpful, but going over things again and again is probably not helpful. This is sometimes called ruminating or even prevarication and it can keep people stuck and unable to make progress. It can also be a form of avoidance — thinking about change rather than actually getting on and doing it. But checking your answers is part of planning, and that is a good idea.

My most important reasons to change drinking are:
1
2
3

My main goals are:
(This is where you put in as much detail as you can and make it as clear as you can — vague statements aren't useful.)
1
2
3

The things I need to do to achieve these goals are:
(Put here some of the practical changes you will need to make to achieve your goals.)
1
2
3

Who can help and how:
(It can be very helpful to enlist other people in your plan. You might need to get over the embarrassment of admitting you are having problems — there is more on this later in the book — but for many people it is an important barrier to overcome)

Possible difficulties and how to overcome or minimize them:

1

2

3

Start date. This is the day on which I am going to make the changes I have planned.

Review date. This is the date on which I am going to take an honest and detailed look at my plan and see if it is working and if it needs to change in any way.

Figure 22 (*continued*)   Summarising Your Plan

Congratulations!

If you have got this far through the book then it is clear that you are serious! You have covered a lot of ground. The first task was to take a long, hard and honest look at your alcohol consumption and what it may be doing to you and the people around you. You have looked at some of the issues you may face in trying to change and understanding that it is not as straightforward as a simple win-or-lose situation. There are probably some very good reasons why drinking has become so central in your life and changing may not always be simple (though for some it can be). There have been some psychological models to grapple with and the conclusions from these theories may not be clear cut. The medical information may have been unsettling and worrying.

If you have been following the programme suggested in this chapter then the stage you are at now is that you have a plan for change. Hopefully, you are happy that it is a realistic and practical plan and you have an intention to try it out and give it a go. The next few pages contain some suggestions that you can use either to check your plan in advance or to help review it afterwards. The approach we are following is called controlled drinking. Some people believe that if you have a drinking problem then abstinence is the only realistic possibility. There is plenty of evidence, however, that this is not always the case. But controlled drinking is not the same as social drinking and we will come back to that in part three. For the moment we will just say that controlled drinking is something that may not seem natural at first and has to be learnt. It is about learning to drink in a new way.

When to Drink

It may seem a bit strange to have a section on changing drinking with a heading about when you drink. But one of the most important decisions you will have to make in practice is actually when to drink (assuming you haven't decided to cut out alcohol altogether). You will have to do this regardless of whether you drink frequently or infrequently. It is important to get this right because so much drinking is influenced by habit — habits that you will need to change.

Having already monitored your own drinking, you know well by now what your patterns of drinking are and when you drink too much. Deciding carefully when to drink, with whom and where, and then sticking to these choices may be enough by itself to help you achieve your goals.

There are 4 things to think about:

1. People
2. Places
3. Times
4. Risk Factors

1   People

Are there familiar faces for heavy drinking? Do you always drink with the same people? It can be more difficult to control your drinking with some people. Sometimes just being with a certain person or group of people acts a cue for drinking. Choose carefully whether and when to drink at all with these guys!

2   Places

Again, familiarity can mean risk! Simply avoid or limit drinking in places where you usually drink too much.

3   Times

When are you planning to start drinking, and how long for? If you are going to have a drink it is usually best to plan it in advance rather than drink spontaneously. This way you can make sure you choose a time when it is easier to control your intake.

4   Other Risk Factors for you

What else leads you to drink too much, including how you feel?

When You're Drinking

There are lots of things you can do to reduce the amount of alcohol you consume and the likelihood of experiencing problems when you actually drink.

We suggest four techniques that might be useful to control your drinking:
- Communicate
- Limit
- Switch
- Slow

Alcohol counsellors call these 'CLaSS' and say that 'it is important to keep your CLASS.'

CLaSS

Communicate your drinking intentions to those you are with early on, so as to make it easier and less awkward when refusing drinks. You also need to be good at refusal, and practice really does help develop skills!

Limit the amount of alcohol you want to drink and stick to your limit. Sometimes having a range (e.g., 4–6 drinks) might help to allow flexibility. If so, aim for the lower limit, and decide not to exceed the upper limit.

Switch to drinks containing fewer units of alcohol. Examples include opting for a lower strength of beer, move from a larger to a smaller glass of wine, or have a single rather than a double measure of spirits.

Slow down — there is no need to drink so quickly! This may be easier said than done as you may have (without realising it) developed a regular pace of drinking. Time yourself with a typical drink in a typical situation and then decide by how much you need to slow down.

The essential thing when you are drinking is to not say to yourself 'it doesn't really matter how much I am drinking,' for two reasons.

Firstly, you know that it really does matter; that's exactly why you are reading this now and don't allow the effects of having had a few drinks hoodwink you into thinking that it doesn't matter.

Secondly, change may be easier said than done, and can take practice and hard work. Thinking it doesn't matter how much you drink may be precisely what led you to heavy drinking in the first place. It may be part of the reason you learned to drink in an uncontrolled way, and, if so, may take some unlearning. This can take time and may need to be approached gradually.

Some Examples in Practice

Judy

Let's assume that Judy has decided that she really is drinking too much after all and wants to cut down. She has been through the exercises and has decided on the following goal. Instead of drinking half a bottle of wine Monday to Friday, she is only going to drink on Friday nights and occasionally when she is out with friends at the weekend. For her, the CLaSS system makes complete sense.

Communicate: She has a talk with her husband. They agree that they will do an experiment and try it for one week and review.

Limit: They agree to have no more than one bottle of wine per week between them. If they go out with friends at the weekend, they will set themselves a limit and they will count their units. They thought about downloading an app for their phone to help them do this, but in the end decided that a small note-book might be simpler and a bit more discrete.

Switch: They are not going to change strength, but they are going to change the type of wine they drink. They plan to go a bit up market and decide to buy their wine from a different shop, which has a greater variety.

Slow down: They will do this by drinking only with a meal and using smaller size wine glasses.

Rob

It's all a bit trickier for Rob. He doesn't communicate that much with anyone and there is no one he feels comfortable telling that he is drinking too much. He decides to give a Drinkline a call. He feels they understand him quite well, but after the first call he feels upset and he doesn't want to ring them back for another chat. Then he has a brainwave. It's a bit unusual but he thinks it might work. He writes down his plan, puts it in an envelope and posts it to himself. He also sets a reminder on his phone that goes off at 7.00pm everyday with a simple message summarising his goal to reduce drinking.

Rob sets himself the limit of no more than two cans each day. The easiest way for him to do this is to make sure he has no money to buy drink. Rob doesn't have much money anyway and what he does have arrives fortnightly. He plans to use his money as soon as he gets it to buy groceries and also buy cans of soft drinks and bottles of water. He intends to switch from beer to coke and water. By mixing up drinks he can slow down the total amount of alcohol he is consuming. The prompts he sets on his phone and the letter he sent to him-self in the post turn out to be very useful reminders.

Sian

Sian is clear what she has to do. She communicates to her friend that there is no way she wants to put herself in a risky situation again. They agree that they will limit their alcohol when they go out by making sure that they don't start drinking early and wait until they get to their destination (a club or party). Switching drinks is definitely part of the plan. Cider is out of the question and all spirits are to be drunk with a mixer. This will help to slow down the con-sumption. But she has another plan as well. She has spotted that she drinks faster when she is dancing, when it is hot, when she is standing up and when the music is loud. So her plan is to only drink alcohol when she is sitting down. When she is dancing or standing in a crowded space she will only drink water.

Eleanor

Eleanor needs a proper chat with her doctor. The place to start is with some clear two-way communication. Then she can make a plan and set herself some limits. She may need to switch a few things such as alcohol and tablets until she gets it right.

Henry

Henry has a complicated set of problems to deal with. When we left him in chapter 3, he was hovering between pre-contemplation (not thinking he had a problem) and contemplation (deciding to talk to a few mates at work). It is going to take some work before he gets to the action phase.

A good start is communication. Henry had started a conversation about getting in shape with his work mate. He thinks that if he is able to set himself some goals and tell his friends about them then they may show some interest and ask him how he is getting on (which could be very useful to him). He will need to set some limits and to do this it might be useful for him to do some counting. He could count the number of units he drinks each week, how many calories he consumes or how much he spends. It doesn't matter which option/method he decides on as long as he does it regularly. Switching is probably going to be tricky for him. He has noticed that drinking beer in the pub can be quite a problem and this is where most of the excess consumption happens. This is not that surprising as the pub has always been associated, for him, with drinking heavily (with his mates when he was young and with work mates more recently), whereas sipping wine with his girlfriend is not that different from having the occasional glass with his parents which was always much more controlled. Henry's target needs to be the pub drinking. He can change the type of beer he drinks and use a whole range of slow-drinking techniques to reduce. Slow-drinking techniques (also called controlled drinking) can be very helpful and we will discuss them fully later on.

What If You Have Decided Not to Drink at All?

For some people, it will feel right to just decide not to drink at all. We know that the more serious your drinking problems are, the more difficult it will be for you to successfully learn and maintain controlled drinking. If you have decided that your problems are really serious, then it might be a good idea to check out some of the earlier tips on controlled drinking to see whether they can be adapted to work for you.

If you have already tried controlled drinking and it has not been successful, then you need to understand the reasons for this, and decide what to do next. The more difficulty you have with controlled drinking, the more you will need to give serious consideration to the bigger change that giving up altogether involves. If you decide to give up altogether you should make sure that you have read the information on alcohol withdrawal earlier in the book.

Talking It Through with Someone Else

Making decisions about changing your drinking may not be easy, and it may be helpful to talk through your situation with someone else. Here are some options:

Your partner
A friend
Your doctor
A member of your family
A counsellor
A telephone helpline (such as <u>DRINKLINE</u>)

The Drinkline helpline offers confidential, accurate, consistent information and advice on sensible drinking to anyone concerned about alcohol misuse, including people with alcohol problems, their families, friends and carers.
   Telephone 0800 917 8282
   (Mon–Fri, 9am–11pm; Sat–Sun, 6pm–11pm)

Who do you think it would be useful to talk about your decision with?
   Write their name and number below and think about when would be a good time to speak to them:

Name :   Tel. No:

It can also be useful to think about what you might say in advance and if, in the future, you would like them to ask you how things are going.
   It can be helpful, too, if someone else knows what you are doing (it can be more of a commitment as well).

Your Plan

Having already monitored your own drinking, you know well by now what your particular patterns of drinking are and when you drink too much. Deciding carefully, when to drink, with whom and where, and then sticking to these choices may be enough by itself to help you achieve your goals. As part of your plan you should also set yourself a review date.

R-Day — The Day When You Review Your Plan and How It Is Going!

On the review date, ask yourself 'How did it go?' Be honest with yourself. Imagine that you are going to be appraised by your boss at work or explaining yourself in court. If you were in a situation like that then you would want to have made some very careful preparations before the meeting. It helps enormously with tasks like this to write your thoughts down in as much detail as you can and then read through your notes and see what you think. How is the plan really measuring up to your hopes and expectations? Are you on target?

Your Drinking Diary (Also Called Your Thinking Drinking Record)

Many people find keeping a regular record of their drinking really helpful. It can be one of the key tools to help you keep track of your drinking. Of course, it is important to be honest when you fill it in. Also, it is best to complete it as close to the time you were drinking as possible. In chapter 2 you had the opportunity to use a record to reflect on how much you were drinking in the past. You can use the same approach to record your drinking in the present.

There are lots of ways to do this. You can try the online tools and apps mentioned in chapter 2. Or you can use a notebook or just enter the data into your own diary or calendar on your phone. The vital information is the number of units you drank each day. You can also add other information to make the record more interesting and helpful. For example, you could record the amount you spent, calories consumed, who you drank with, how you felt, where you drank and what you did while or after you were drinking.

With the information from your drinking diary you will be well placed to answer the following questions on your Review Day.

How Well are You Doing?

After you've used your thinking drinking record and thought about how it's all been going, there are two possible things to do. We suggest you do both as they are both likely to be helpful:

1. Celebrate the successes! Do this if everything has gone well, or and also if, some things did go well and some things didn't. Both are real achievements and you have good reason to feel satisfied. Be good to yourself . . . but without drinking!
2. Learn from what was difficult and the things that have not gone so well. These experiences provide valuable material for gaining further control over your drinking. Whether they will be useful to you depends upon how you use them. Persistence really is a virtue and pays off in behaviour change.

Decision Time

You now have an important decision to make: whether to carry on with the plan exactly as it was, or whether you need to modify it. If things have gone well, there may not be much reason to change the plan.

If you do decide to alter your change plan, however, there are two things that you might do:

1. It may be useful to return to Part 1 to check out how you came to this particular plan in the first place. Ask yourself whether this was the right plan for you at this time.
2. However, you may well be clear about your reasons for choosing a particular plan of action. If the reasons are good ones then it is likely to be the detail of your plan that may not be working for you. In this case, we suggest that you examine these details and think about adapting or changing them.

The chapters that follow are designed to help you carry out your plan with some very practical ideas to help you achieve your goals.

CHAPTER 6

Putting Your Plan into Action

Turning a good intention into a pattern of behaviour that you can stick to no matter what takes skill as well as determination. Resolutions genuinely made on New Year's Eve (even when sober) rarely make it much longer than mid January. Whether it is reducing drinking, going to the gym, sticking to a diet or giving up on an unhealthy relationship makes little difference. To be successful you will need some sensible, practical strategies and common sense as well as resolve and willpower.

In chapter 5 we looked at strategies that will help you to reduce the number of times you are at risk of drinking. In this chapter we focus on the nitty gritty of handling situations when you are actually confronted with more booze than you had planned for and you need to deal with it.

Refusing Drinks and Being Assertive

For some people drinking is a social activity – drinking in the pub, with meals, at a party, etc. In this type of situation, you are likely to be offered a drink. Saying 'no' can be difficult. You might not want to offend or might feel embarrassed. Even if you fully intend not to have more than a couple of drinks, it can still be difficult to turn an offer down.

It is easier to refuse drinks if you have prepared and practiced beforehand.

Preparing and Practicing Beforehand

Imagine a situation when someone offers you a drink and you think you shouldn't accept it. Have you thought about what you might say? It can be very helpful to have planned for this situation in advance.

You might want to have a script ready, something you can say that is short, snappy and really clear, but is not rude or unpleasant. You might also be able to avoid drinking without using words. For example, if you are in a restaurant and you see someone picking up a bottle and moving it towards your glass you might quietly move your glass away. Or, in a pub with a group of friends you might choose to leave (perhaps to go the toilet) if you think someone is about to buy a round of drinks.

Explaining You Don't Want a Drink

Another situation might be if someone pushes you to have drink. You can explain why you don't want to drink, although you don't have to give an explanation. You can just say 'no.' But if you do wish to respond, it is best to make it brief and not get involved in long explanations or justifications.

> Sometimes we give long explanations to justify things to ourselves more than trying to persuade someone else. A long explanation has risks. It might encourage other people to ask questions or they may make comments that could be unhelpful.

Refusal Skills

Saying 'no' to a drink is not always easy especially if you are not used to saying no. It takes some getting used to, but it is a skill that can be practiced, and practicing helps.

What If Someone Tries to Hand You a Drink?

A polite assertive 'no, thank you' may be all you need to say, or having a drink already in your hand might put them off offering you another one.

> You don't have to have a drink because it is offered to you.
>   This may seem strange at first because the culture around us often encourages us to drink as much as possible. Pub, hotel, restaurant and club owners want you to drink plenty, and the profits of the alcohol industry depend on it. Supermarkets and off-licenses have special offers on drinks. Even the government does well out the tax revenue.

It is also possible to 'lose' drinks. You can just put a drink down and walk away. Or you can pretend you are drinking more than you really are. And it is always useful to have a response ready, such as:

'No thanks, I don't drink anymore.'
'No thanks, I'm driving.'
'No thanks, I'm on a diet.'
'No thanks, I drink too much'
'No thanks, I've got an early start tomorrow morning'
'No thanks, I'm on medication'
'No thanks, it makes me sick'
'No thanks, I'm training'

> Saying 'no' to a drink can go against the grain. We might feel like we are missing out on an opportunity or depriving ourselves, but that is the old-style thinking that we are trying to change.

Or perhaps we don't want to appear rude and turn down someone's offer. It can be very difficult to refuse drinks when you are with other people who are drinking.

If you go somewhere with someone, agree beforehand that you will leave if you feel uncomfortable.

> Sometimes people may encourage you to drink a lot in order to disguise their own heavy drinking. They don't feel quite so bad about their own drinking if it seems that other people are drinking at the same rate as them — try to avoid falling for that one!

Planning Ahead

So what can you say? Use this form to plan ahead (it would be good to plan for up to three situations):

---

1. Situation
   What would be a skilled way to handle this situation?

   What could you say or do?

2. Situation
   What would be a skilled way to handle this situation?

   What could you say or do?

3. Situation
   What would be a skilled way to handle this situation?

   What could you say or do?

Figure 23   Planning Ahead Form

Assertiveness

You might be thinking 'why is there a section on assertiveness in a book about drinking?' It is here because lots of people say that when they are frustrated or angry they turn to drink. Or perhaps they are fed up with feeling stepped on and taken for granted, so they drink. Also, refusing drinks takes assertiveness to carry out. Assertiveness is about being more effective.

Being assertive is not the same as being aggressive. Many people become aggressive when they drink too much. Quite often people become aggressive when they have failed to be assertive so they become aggressive instead. Being able to get your point across in a strong, but reasonable, way is usually more effective than screaming or shouting or, worse still, using physical violence.

Assertiveness Is an Attitude

Assertiveness is an attitude and a way of relating to the outside world, backed up by the skills needed for effective communication. To be truly assertive, you need to see yourself as being of worth and as having a right to enjoy life. At the same time, you value others equally, respecting their right to an opinion and to enjoy themselves.

While some people think that being assertive is about being selfish, it is in fact the opposite. Assertiveness is about acknowledging that all opinions are important. An assertive attitude says 'I matter and you do too.'

It's the Way You Say It!

There are many things you can do to learn to become more assertive:

Assertive communication: It isn't just the content of what you say that counts, it is also the way you put it across. It helps to be honest with yourself about your own feelings, to keep calm and stick to the point, to be clear, specific and direct.

> People don't always go along with what you want or see things from your point of view. If they did then we wouldn't have to be assertive. So it is helpful to be able to deal with their objections.

If you meet objections from other people, there are some techniques you can try:

- Keep repeating your message while also listening to the other's point of view (this is sometimes called the *broken record technique*).
- Try to offer alternative solutions if you can
- Ask, if you are unsure about something
- If the other person tries to create a diversion, point this out calmly and repeat your message
- Use appropriate body language
- Always respect the rights and point of view of the other person

Practicing and Preparation

It is worthwhile thinking about things in advance, especially if you think a situation might be difficult. For example, you may want to plan to be assertive in certain work situations, such as refusing to accept additional work. In a situation like this, you could plan what you might say, such as 'I'd be delighted to help you with that piece of work, but we'll need to agree what I'm going to drop as I don't have time to do it all.'

Risky Situations: Managing the Where, When and Who of Drinking

One of the main skills to learn is how to avoid situations in which you are most likely to drink. We covered this in part 1 and if you missed this exercise (or forgotten what was covered) you may wish to go back to it now. The key thing is to keep away from tricky situations and also to be able to handle risky ones as they come up.

Keeping Away from Tricky Situations

For the most part, this is reasonably obvious. But it is much easier to say what to do than actually do it. If you know that you always drink heavily with a particular person, or in a particular place, then it is best to keep away from these situations as much as possible. However, if the person is your partner or friend and the place is your home or local pub, then you may have a problem.

As we have mentioned quite a few times before, planning ahead is very helpful. For example, it may make sense to arrange to meet at a place where there is no alcohol or where you don't usually drink that much. Ensuring that there is no alcohol around at home (even for guests or 'medicinal purposes') is usually a good idea.

Filling in the table below may help you start on this:

Situations to Avoid	Alternatives

Figure 24   Situations to Avoid and Alternatives

Handling Risky Situations

There are 4 common types of risky situation to think about:

1. Where there are negative feelings
2. Where there are conflicts between people
3. Where there is social pressure
4. Where there are positive feelings

We will look briefly at each of these in turn and think about how you might deal with them.

1. Where situations lead you to feel negative emotions, such as:
   anger
   frustration
   anxiety
   depression
   boredom
   What situations do you encounter that fit this description?

   What ways can you deal with them that don't involve alcohol?

2. Where conflicts between people mean you are more likely to drink: These might be full-blown rows or conflicts that just simmer for a long time but never get properly addressed.
   What situations do you encounter that fit this description?

   What ways can you deal with them that don't involve alcohol?

3. When social pressure means you are more likely to drink: This could be clear and obvious pressure to drink or the more subtle expectancy that you will drink, such as when you are with people who are determined to get drunk or, perhaps, just tipsy. Or the social pressure might not have anything to do with alcohol, but you feel uncomfortable so you drink.
   What situations do you encounter that fit this description?

   What ways can you deal with them that don't involve alcohol?

4. When having positive feelings mean that you are more likely to drink: These could be celebrations, relief at having completed a difficult task or enjoying yourself and feeling relaxed.
   What situations do you encounter that fit this description?

   What ways can you deal with them that don't involve alcohol?

Controlled Drinking (Drinking to a Target)

We have already mentioned this idea briefly. Many people set themselves a target of drinking only a certain amount of alcohol each day or each week. As we have seen, this is often called controlled drinking, and it is important to recognise that this is a skill that may have to be learned. Quite often people have a history of uncontrolled drinking and that is why they seek help to change their drinking. Drinking in a controlled way may not come naturally.

Controlled drinking is not the same as social drinking, although it may look the same to someone watching you. There is a big difference between social drinkers and controlled drinkers. Although both types of drinkers may consume similar amounts of alcohol, they do so in different ways and for different reasons. Social drinkers do it naturally; controlled drinkers have to work at it!

Many former heavy drinkers have the goal of becoming social drinkers — and they are often able to achieve this — but it might take a while to get there.

Social Drinkers	Controlled Drinkers
• Don't plan their drinking in advance • May drink in rounds • Sometimes get drunk • Don't bother to carefully count their drinks	• Plan in advance and drink to a target • Always get their own drinks • Never get drunk • Always know how much they have drunk and are going to drink

Figure 25   Social Versus Controlled Drinking

It might seem as if controlled drinking takes all the fun and spontaneity out of drinking — well, that's true to some extent, but it can also be seen as a helpful (and perhaps necessary) stage towards a more relaxed, satisfying approach to alcohol in your life.

Practical Strategies

It is common for people to drink in a habitual way. Many people have automatic drinking habits that lead them to consume excessive amounts of alcohol. So the aim of this section is to help you break your old drinking habits and develop some new (more helpful) ones.

Slowing Down

Many people who drink too much find they also drink very quickly. They take large gulps, don't taste their drink, always keep their glass in their hand, and fill their glasses to the brim (well nearly). Drinking quickly can be very dangerous to health and can (in severe cases) be fatal.

Take a moment to think about the habitual ways you drink. It might be helpful to write them down. Are you someone who stands at the bar drinking, sits in a chair at home with a glass in your hand watching the TV, walks along the street with a can, only drinks with a meal, only drinks with your best mate? You will need to know what your habits are so you can change them.

Here are some ideas that people have found helpful:

• Alternate alcohol with a soft drink or a weaker drink
• Pour smaller measures at home

- Have two days a week when you don't drink at all
- Drink water (or a non-alcoholic drink) and eat well before starting to drink alcohol
- Put your glass down between sips
- Hold the glass with your other hand
- Position the glass or bottle some distance away so it is difficult to reach easily
- Avoid drinking in rounds and always get your own drinks
- Eat something alongside drinking (not salty things like crisps or nuts)
- Sit down when drinking (people tend to drink more when standing, especially in pubs or clubs)
- Drink with people who usually drink less than you do
- Drink in a place where you don't usually drink or usually drink only a little
- Pace your drinking — spread your drinks out
- Time your drinks (with the aim of slowing down as the time progresses)

Which strategies do you think you will find most useful? Write them in the box below along with your thoughts about when and where you can use them. We have started you off with a couple of examples — you fill in the rest.

Strategy	When, who, where etc	How I will use it
Putting my glass beyond easy reach and not fill my glass to the top	Watching TV at home	I will put the bottle back in the fridge, only half fill the glass and put the glass on the sideboard on the other side of the room and not on the coffee table
Avoid alcoholic drinks altogether	Night out at the pub and then on to a friend's house	I will drink soft drinks only, arrive at the pub later than everyone else, eat a big meal before setting off, sit down and not join in rounds. If I feel tempted to drink I will go home early.

Figure 26   Slowing Down Strategies

A Couple of New Case Studies

We are going to look at a couple of hard cases now. As before, they are fictional characters, but they have been introduced so you can see how some of the suggestions in this chapter might work out in practice. And we have chosen hard cases because we know that change can be difficult sometimes and dealing with hard problems can show what is involved.

Jim's Story

Jim is 37 years old. He is ex-army, ex-police and a few months ago he became an ex-husband. His ex-wife wanted him to become an ex-father as well, but Jim wasn't having it. He was determined to keep in contact with both his kids and he fought hard for this. It was a matter of principle to him, a matter of pride that he wasn't going to let his kids think that he was a lousy father or, worse still, he didn't want them to call his ex-wife's new boy friend 'dad.' He'd had the same battle to keep in touch with the kids from his other family as well. His first marriage had been in his early twenties and that hadn't worked out either.

Alcohol had played a part in both of the breakups. Jim had started drinking at around 13 and, by 17, he was drinking regularly and quite heavily. After joining the army, he slowed down a bit, until he returned from his first tour of duty abroad where he'd been involved in several combat situations. On the way back to their base in the UK, his unit had a period of 'de-stressing' — another name for a prolonged drinking session on the beach! This was followed by a rest period back at their base where the alcohol was cheap (subsidized) and plentiful. The attitude of their commanding officer was that the boys had been through a very rough time and deserved a good drink if they wanted one.

The impact of all this drinking was catastrophic for his young family. He was rarely at home and when he was there he was often bad tempered and tired. Family breakup after active service is not unusual in the armed services and after the divorce the drink really got a hold. Jim was also getting fed up with the military lifestyle and he took the first opportunity he could to leave the army. It was hard for him to adapt to his new life and, although he found work as a civilian in the police force for a while, he left that as well after a few months. It was whilst working for the police that he met his most recent wife. At first he cut down on the drinking, but he was bored at home (babies and toddlers bored him) and he began to regularly drift down to the pub. He was not sure when his wife started to see someone else, but as soon as he found out about it he left.

The turning point came when he found himself living in a bedsit, depressed and sick. He'd had some stomach pains and the doctor had enquired about drinking. For the first time in his life Jim seriously questioned his alcohol intake. The doctor put Jim in touch with a specialist alcohol nurse that came to the surgery once a week. He had a few confidential sessions with the nurse and Jim trusted him. At the nurse's suggestion Jim kept an alcohol diary and together they agreed on the target of drinking 20 units a week. The nurse gave Jim a self-help booklet on reducing drinking to take home and suggested he try out some of the suggestions in the booklet. They would discuss how Jim got on at their weekly appointments.

The main issue for Jim was lager. He had drunk gallons of the stuff over the years and he liked it — a lot. Jim could not imagine going to the pub and only drinking one or two pints. And if he didn't go to the pub he did not know what he would do with himself during the evenings and weekends. The plan was as follows: go to the pub less often and drink less when he did go to the pub. Here are the specifics:

1. Only go to the pub on three or four days each week. On other days visit friends or family in their own homes. This included seeing his kids and taking them out (he wouldn't drink in front of his children).
2. When he does go for a drink, avoid pubs where his ex-army friends are (he can see them in their own homes if he wishes).
3. Stop drinking lager — try other beers.
4. Eat before going out and arrive later in the evening.
5. Always sit at a table a long way from the bar. Buy his own drinks and don't accept drinks from other people or drink in rounds.
6. Tell his mates that he has to drink less because he is on tablets from the doctor (which was true).

This plan worked really well — for three weeks! Jim kept to his plan at first, and he was pleased and proud of his achievements. He thought he had really cracked it and was optimistic about the future. So when things started to slip Jim was really disappointed and upset. The alcohol nurse at the practice wasn't fazed though. He seen this before and knew that although the techniques were great they weren't enough on their own. However, they had shown Jim that change was possible and he had not known that before. So that had been a good place to start. Although Jim was well motivated to change, his attitude towards alcohol hadn't changed much and this would need some attention as well. Jim wasn't drinking as much as he used to, so there were some gaps in his life to fill. He also viewed alcohol as the solution to his problems rather than the cause of some of them. The psychological strategies for dealing with these issues are discussed in the next section. But we have another case study to work through first.

Julie's Story

Our second case is Julie. Her drinking had only got out of hand in the last six months, but she had been drinking regularly for years. Julie's usual pattern was to go to the pub with some of the other teachers from her school after work every Friday. They would meet up at about 6.00 pm, have a few glasses of wine, and then go home to their families and their weekends. This had suited her well. Her partner usually had dinner ready and they would settle down to an evening of more wine and a smoke (cannabis). The drinking had increased with the increasing stress at school. The combination of a new and rather bossy head of department and a disappointing OFSTED report had created an atmosphere of distrust and suspicion amongst the staff. There was more and more paperwork to complete, extra meetings and lessons were being observed by senior staff. Julie used to enjoy her work, but now she felt unhappy and found that she had little time to spend with the pupils outside of lessons. She brought marking home and spent at least two of her evenings at home each week on the computer writing up her lesson plans. The Friday nights in the pubs were now spent talking about work and Julie had begun to feel anxious that her boss was keeping an eye on her performance.

Most nights she and her partner had drunk a glass of wine with their meal. Now she had an extra glass as she did the marking. She talked a lot to her partner about what was happening at school, but after a while she began to worry that she was boring him so she became quieter and more introverted. After finishing the marking, she often felt quite wound up and couldn't sleep so she would have a smoke to calm herself down. Drinking at the weekends increased and she stopped doing things she enjoyed such as seeing friends, going shopping and playing badminton at the local sport centre on Saturday mornings. Julie was becoming depressed!

The turning point came when a colleague at work took her to one side and asked her what was the matter. It all came pouring out and Julie decided that she needed to take some action. She could see that her drinking was not helping and was actually making things worse. Her friend suggested that she go online and find out what she could do to help herself. Julie found a website with an alcohol drinks calculator and to her astonishment calculated that she was drinking around 25 units a week (plus the cannabis). Julie did a lot of reading and worked out a plan for herself. She communicated (talked) with her friend and agreed a plan that limited her to just drinking on Friday nights. She bought a large supply of cans of coke and chocolate, and switched to these on weekdays. She also planned to go to the gym regularly to deal with any potential problems with her weight resulting from all the high-sugar foods. This was all a good plan, but it wasn't going to work that well unless she also did something about the pressure at work. She talked it over with her friends at the pub the following Friday. Together they went to see the head of department. This meeting did not go well and they had a bit of a row. However, Julie was able to say what had been on her mind and she decided that she would start looking for a job in a different school. Julie was very angry and upset about all of this, but the drinking was now back under control.

Summary

Changing *how much* you drink usually involves changing *the way* you drink. When it comes to putting a plan into action there will undoubtedly be challenges on the way. You will probably face situations in which you have to say 'no' when offered a drink, resist all kinds of temptation and have to deal with the reasons that underlie your heavy drinking.

You are not the first to make this journey and others have been generous enough to share things they have learned along the way. Some of them are listed here as 'Top Tips'. Have a read and make a note of the ones you think may be useful to you. You may want to come back to the list and read them again at a later date. There are lots of ways to keep these tips in your mind. You could write them on 'post it' notes and stick them on the fridge door, in your diary or next to the drinks cabinet. Enter them into the calendar function on your phone and have them pop up as reminders every day. Put them on your screen saver. Perhaps you can think of other ways to do this — the key thing is to keep them fresh and relevant to you and your particular situation.

Top Tips

1. Count units as you go along rather than add them up at the end of the day
2. Set yourself a daily target and stick to it
3. If you know you might have an alcoholic drink make sure you have something to eat beforehand (carbohydrates are especially good)
4. If you are thirsty drink water not alcohol
5. Alternate soft drinks with alcoholic drinks
6. Drink lots of water throughout the day
7. Put your glass down between drinks
8. Don't drink every day — have a gap of at least one or two days each week
9. Have drinks with lower alcohol content
10. Avoid drinking in rounds
11. Don't top your glass up as you go along — be clear how much you are drinking
12. If you drink at home recycle your bottles or cans each week and count how many you have used
13. Don't socialise with heavy drinkers
14. Ask someone you trust to keep an eye on how much you are drinking and to remind you to slow down or stop
15. Sip a drink slowly — don't gulp it down in large mouthfuls
16. Be careful with mixers — they can disguise how much you are drinking
17. Read the label on the bottle or can and see how strong the drink actually is
18. Avoid strong lagers, beers, wines, etc, — drink normal strength
19. Watch out for homebrews — they can be much stronger than you think
20. Coffee or tea does not help you sober up — it just disguises the effects alcohol is having on your body

21. Alcohol stays in the body a long time so watch out for 'topping up' effects the next day
22. Drinking alcohol can lead to bad decision making
23. If you do drink, don't get drunk
24. Pace your drinking and use a watch to time your drinks
25. Don't forget to say 'no thanks' if offered a drink
26. Avoid situations or places where you usually drink
27. If you are finding it difficult to control your drinking, discuss it with a friend
28. Plan how much you are going to drink in advance and stick to the plan
29. Always start with a non-alcoholic drink
30. Don't have a drink when (or because) you feel upset or angry
31. Don't have a drink when (or because) you feel bored
32. Don't go out to 'have a drink' — go out for another reason that doesn't involve alcohol
33. Sit down when you drink alcohol — people who drink standing up tend to drink more
34. Have something in your hands other than a glass
35. Don't mix drinks
36. Add up how much money you have saved
37. Don't take much cash with you when drinking and leave your credit card at home
38. Don't borrow money to drink or run up a tab at the bar.

CHAPTER 7

The Way You Think

In the last chapter we saw that both Jim and Laura had to change the way they thought about alcohol to help change their behaviour around drinking. This chapter looks specifically at changes that you might want to make to your thinking that can help support you and help you to stick to your goals

Attitudes

Our attitude towards alcohol and heavy drinking may have big influence on our ability to change or control our drinking. For example, if we feel that we are being forced or persuaded by someone else to change, then we are unlikely to try very hard to change. If, on the other hand, we want to change for our own reasons and we have come to the decision ourselves, then we are likely to be more enthusiastic and give it a good try.

The effects of attitudes can be very subtle. Sometimes we hold an attitude that we aren't really aware of until someone or an event points it out. These are often called *implicit attitudes* and can have quite a big influence on the way we behave. We often don't question these implicit attitudes because they may seem really obvious to us. They are ideas that we take for granted and quite often assume that other people feel and think the same way that we do.

One way to find out more about the kinds of attitudes people hold towards drinking alcohol is to conduct surveys. Social attitudes surveys ask people about their attitudes towards drinking. Some typical questions are reproduced below. Try answering the questions for yourself to see what *you* think about drinking — not just your own drinking but other peoples' drinking as well. The implicit attitudes you hold are quite likely to influence how you go about setting goals for yourself. There aren't any right or wrong answers to these questions — it's all a matter of opinion (and attitude)!

A lot of people I know would think it odd if I didn't drink alcohol at all. Is that true in your situation? How do you know what people would think?

Some people say that if you allow pubs and bars to stay open for longer people will simply drink more, others say that longer opening hours will mean that people will pace their drinking more sensibly.

It's easier to enjoy a social event if you've had a drink

Most people with serious drinking problems have only themselves to blame.

Here are some places where people might like to drink alcohol. For each one please tick one box to show whether people should or should not be allowed to drink there.

In a public park?	allowed ○	not allowed ○
At a football match?	allowed ○	not allowed ○
In the street?	allowed ○	not allowed ○
On trains?	allowed ○	not allowed ○

Figure 27   Attitudes Towards Drinking

Getting drunk is a perfectly acceptable thing to do at weekends. What do you think of this?

Drinking is a major part of most people's way of life. Do you think this is true? If you think it is true, do you think this is a good thing?

Leaving aside whether it's legal or not, do you personally think it is wrong or not wrong for a fourteen-year-old to drink a small amount of alcohol at home with their parents, as long as they don't get drunk?

Always wrong	○
Mostly wrong	○
Sometimes wrong	○
Rarely wrong	○
Not wrong at all	○

Figure 28   Where You Drink Questionnaire; Do You Think Teenage Drinking
Is Wrong?

There are not any correct answers to these questions, but it is very useful to know what your attitudes are as they will influence how and when you drink alcohol. Attitudes can be held weakly or strongly and can be fixed or flexible. If they are very rigid then it can be hard to make changes that last; if they are too flexible then it might be hard to get the determination to actually make a change and stick to it.

After you have thought about your attitudes towards drinking alcohol it might be helpful to list those attitudes that would support you in achieving your drinking goals and those that would be unhelpful.

Which attitudes are helpful and which are unhelpful?

You could also make a list of those attitudes that are not helpful and think about how you could change them. You might want to change an attitude or perhaps you could try and hold them less strongly.

A Few Brief Examples

Jane

Jane travels a lot for work. She has a senior management role in a large company and she attends meetings up and down the country and often stays at hotels. Her attitude towards alcohol is that it is a normal part of her business life. After meetings she will drink with colleagues to relax and to oil the wheels of conversations. She assumes that her colleagues are comfortable with regular drinking so never questions it. She will routinely order a bottle of wine at dinner with colleagues and would be surprised if anyone objected. In fact, she would think they were being rude. There are regular celebrations at work: birthdays, good quarterly results, leaving dos. These occasions always involve quite a bit to drink. As far as Jane is concerned this level of drinking is normal.

Dr. Jenkins

Dr. Jenkins has a taste for single malt whiskey. He has a large collection at home and has a large glass every night before bed. His attitude is that drinking malts shows how refined he is and is a sign of his status. He believes that it is OK for him to drink a lot because (he tells himself) 'as a medical man' he is aware of the effects of alcohol on the body and knows when to stop. He thinks that the medical profession has got it wrong when it advises only 21 units a week for men. He 'knows' that he has a strong metabolism and can handle his alcohol. He is not, after all, a lightweight. He was rather shocked when he was later diagnosed with liver disease!

Kevin

Kevin believed that all journalists drink heavily and that it was an essential part of the job to train himself to drink without showing anyone that he was drunk. He thought that hanging around in wine bars and clubs would be a good way to make contacts and pick up stories.

Joe

Joe played darts for the local pub team. It was a part of the culture to drink several pints of beer on darts nights. So he did. He thought that if he didn't drink heavily the others would think he wasn't 'a proper man'. He knew this was a bit of a stereotyped view of pubs darts team players, but that didn't make any difference — he still drank.

Ras

Ras came from a religious family that was strongly opposed to drinking alcohol of any kind. He believed that he would bring shame on the family if anyone from his community knew that he'd had a drink. On the other hand, he thought that his mates would look down on him if he didn't drink at all. Ras was in a real conflict. He tried to hide his drinking and he had difficulty learning how to control it. Mostly he wouldn't drink, but when he did have a drink he ended up very drunk and ill. He couldn't go home in that state so spent the night sleeping on his friends' floors. He invented some excuses for his family and eventually left home.

Marie

Marie was at home with a young baby. She wasn't coping well and was tired and tearful much of the time. She believed that she should be someone who coped perfectly and didn't need help. Marie wouldn't touch even a single glass of wine. She was frightened that if she drank any alcohol at all she would completely collapse and then wouldn't be able to cope at all. She wouldn't accept any help from relatives or friends. It was tough for Marie and she couldn't loosen up.

'Self-efficacy': Do You Believe You Can Change?

This is a very big and important question. Do you really believe you can do things that will affect what happens to you or are you in the hands of fate?

People who believe that they can do things that make a difference tend to feel better about themselves, set themselves more challenging goals, try harder and have more control over their drinking. By contrast, people who doubt themselves, avoid challenges and worry about their failures have a harder time getting to grips with problem drinking. So it makes sense to work on developing attitudes and beliefs that will help you to tackle heavy drinking and achieve your goals.

This is called building up *self-efficacy*. We can develop greater self-efficacy by creating experiences for ourselves which give us an experience of success and mastery. You could try the following exercise.

Set yourself some goals and then give yourself credit when you achieve them. They don't have to be drinking goals. In fact, it is probably easier to steer yourself away from drinking goals at first and try something a little easier. It could be goals at home, work, the gym or at college. It doesn't matter what you try to do — the important thing is to have a go at something.

Then ask yourself how you will give yourself credit when you have achieved it. Quite often we set rather vague goals for ourselves and then we don't know properly when, or if, we have achieved them. And if we don't have a clear outcome then we don't reward ourselves. Rewards are important and sometimes we might hold an attitude that rewards are taboo. There is nothing wrong with acknowledging progress and rewarding ourselves for doing something well as long as the reward is appropriate. So whether it is chocolate, a trip to the cinema, a new piece of clothing or a chat with a friend make sure that you tell yourself how well you have done. Needless to say it is probably best not to use alcohol as a reward!

Talk to yourself positively. Don't spend time worrying about tiny faults. Build yourself up for even the smallest of successes. Remember that it takes energy and effort to succeed. You won't get there straight away.

Role Models

This is about implicit attitudes again. We all tend to have someone we look up to or admire, although we may not be aware of it or admit it! It may be someone famous, from history or from amongst our families and friends. It could be someone who was important to us when we were younger (parent, teacher, youth leader) or someone we know now. These role models can usefully guide us and help us keep going when things are tough. Who would be a good role model for you? It doesn't need to be someone you actually know, but someone who impresses you and who you think you would like to be like (or do something as well as they do).

Being Determined, Thinking Carefully and Treating Yourself Well

One attitude that people sometimes hold is that you have to be tough on yourself if you are going to change your drinking. Well, it is true that changing drinking habits can be tough work, but you don't necessarily have to be tough on yourself to succeed.

You do have to be determined, though. Being determined means that you are serious about change and that you are prepared to put in a lot of effort and put up with some discomfort to achieve your goals. It also means that you are working hard to achieve your goals, and that you are using all your abilities to succeed. It means you are using your intelligence, making careful decisions, asking for help if you need it, putting aside time to prepare for possible problems and being resolute (not allowing setbacks to become failures).

Being determined also means facing up to difficulties as they come along. The difficulties that you face may be from any part of your life. Adopting a determined attitude in the face of these can be very important. Facing up to a problem, rather than avoiding it, can help you deal with it better and usually leads to a better solution. Dealing with a problem means thinking about it and often thinking about it in detail. If the issue we are dealing with is an upsetting one then it is likely that our thinking processes can be thrown into disarray.

What Can Happen to Our Thinking

In chapter 3 we explained that one of the approaches adopted in this book comes from an approach to treatment called cognitive behavioural therapy (CBT). This next section is based strongly on CBT and is about the way strong emotions can distort the way we think about situations we are in. Here are some of the common ways in which our thinking can become distorted:

All-or-nothing thinking: Things can seem to be either good or bad and are never in-between. For example, you might feel that the ideas in this book will either work for you or they won't, or that you are either a heavy drinker or totally abstinent. Another variation could be to think 'if I don't drink alcohol I will never have any pleasure or enjoyment in my life' rather than thinking that you can still enjoy yourself without having a drink. When feeling upset or worried it can be hard to find the middle ground.

Mental filtering or being selective: This involves only paying attention to certain things. An example might be only remembering the times you enjoyed yourself when you were drinking or thinking all your friends drink heavily and forgetting that some of them actually drink only occasionally or moderately.

Over-generalising: This involves taking one event and thinking it applies to lots (or even all) events — e.g., believing that alcohol is always bad in all situations rather than seeing that sometimes having an alcoholic drink can be OK.

Mindreading: This is when you think that other people know what is going on for you. For example, thinking that other people are aware that you are working on changing your drinking habits or that people know you are feeling worried, anxious, depressed, etc.

Beliefs about control: This is when you can't see what is really controlling a situation — e.g., believing that alcohol controls you rather than you control alcohol.

Emotional reasoning: This is when you use your feelings as evidence. Sometimes this can mean that because you feel strongly that something is true it seems to you that it must, therefore, be true.

Predicting the future: This relates to feeling that you know what is going to happen in advance, when, in reality, there is no real way of knowing what will happen. An example might be predicting that you are bound to drink more than your target in a given situation. There is the danger here of the self-fulfilling prophecy — this is when you believe something is going to happen and you end up doing things that make it more likely to happen.

It is quite possible to overcoming distorted thinking. The basic principle is to check out your thoughts against reality. Remind yourself that 'because I think something is the case that doesn't mean it really is the case.' Try using questions to check out your thoughts such as:

• What is the evidence for what I believe?
• Are there any other possible explanations?
• Would somebody else, in my situation, think the same as me?
• What would I advise someone else to do in this situation?

Treating Yourself Well

There are questions posed in this book that may be hard to face. It takes courage to confront a drinking pattern that may have been going on for many years. It can be difficult to take a long, hard, honest look at our pattern of drinking. This can be an upsetting and sometimes painful process. It is important, when we do this, to make sure that we give ourselves a bit of a pat on the back for making the effort and to make sure that we do not think of ourselves in too harsh a manner. It is good to be honest with ourselves, but is also good to be kind to ourselves. We should treat ourselves with some compassion.

Changing drinking can give you the opportunity to change the way you feel about yourself. Instead of harshly judging failures you can be a bit more sympathetic and warm towards yourself. And as long as you remain determined to change then that should be OK. Hopefully, you are experiencing some success in achieving your goals; but if there are problems, then rather than attacking yourself for slipping up, or making excuses for a lapse, you can say to yourself that you are doing your best, that it will take time and that you are making an effort. There can be many things in people's lives that are painful and difficult to deal with. You already know that heavy drinking won't remove them, but neither will being harsh to yourself.

Katie's Story

Katie lost her job three years ago. She had been struggling to keep up with the workload for quite some time and the drinking was becoming more regular.

She was often late for work and had lots of time off sick. It had become obvious to everyone that she was drinking, but no one had said anything. One day she was late back from lunch and her boss smelt alcohol on her breath. She was sacked more or less on the spot.

Katie was mortified! She felt embarrassed and ashamed. She felt that she had let her family down, but more than anything else she felt that she had let herself down. She was very harsh with herself and in her own mind painted herself as a worthless person who couldn't be relied upon or trusted. The result was that she stopped seeing her friends and stayed at home watching daytime TV and drinking. With a low income and a drinking habit, the debts soon mounted up and it wasn't long before she fell behind on her credit card repayments. Katie was in a serious downward spiral and the more she thought about it the more hopeless and useless she felt herself to be.

The change came when she had a chat with an old family friend. He had known her since childhood and he reminded her of all the things she had achieved when she was younger. He didn't praise her or give her false feedback, but he did treat her with respect. This was startling to Katie because she had lost all respect for herself. This friend did more than reminisce about the good times in the past, he talked about all the good qualities that she had — how she had helped people out when they were in trouble, how she had played with the neighbours' children and how she had looked after his cat when he had gone on holiday. These were ordinary things that Katie wasn't thinking about anymore. Katie's attitude towards herself began to change and she began to think less about being a bad person and more about her positive qualities.

Treating yourself kindly does not come easily to many people. We are often encouraged (by parents, teachers, bosses) to be hypercritical of ourselves, especially if we fail to measure up to some very high standard we have set. Whilst we need to be aware of our shortcomings, being highly self-critical is not the best way to make healthy and lasting changes to our behaviour.

One way to be more accepting and friendly to ourselves is to be friendly, accepting and kind to other people. It is the opposite of being cynical, cool or judgmental towards others. Being generous to other people can lead to you feeling more generous towards yourself. When you give other people a bit of leeway, you may find it easier to give yourself some. And actually doing something helpful alongside thinking about it adds some weight to the thoughts — it makes them stronger. So helping out a friend, giving away some of the money you might have otherwise spent on drink, or being friendly to someone can help you to develop a more supportive and accepting view of yourself. There is a growing body of research showing that behaving in a compassionate way and thinking about ourselves in a kindly fashion is actually reflected in the structures of the brain.

Katie's particular difficulty was the shame that she felt. This is what fed the inner voice whispering in her ear that she wasn't really worth bothering with. She couldn't believe that she was a worthwhile person. She felt even worse when she compared herself with other people. It was always a negative comparison in her mind. One way for Katie to improve this could be for her to take a broader view of her situation. Instead of simply blaming herself for her shortcomings, she could say to herself that, while it is true that she has made some mistakes, she didn't do these things on purpose. She hadn't set out to deliberately get into debt, lose her job or alienate her friends. Instead, she could accept that her life was currently in a mess and that she was struggling to sort it out. She could remind herself that a worthless person wouldn't feel bad about the way things were. It is because she has values and standards that it bothers her so much. Coming from this point of view it is easier to accept some help and get on with improving her situation.

There are some similarities between this approach and the AA system in which the first step is to accept that you have a problem. The difference, though, is that for some people abstinence isn't the only solution. And you don't have to feel terrible about yourself for having a drink and staying in control.

Who Is in Control of Your Drinking?

Is it you or the drink? Or are there largely external factors that you can't influence? It is important to know what you really think about these questions. Your attitude to how much you have a say in your behaviour will influence the type of strategies you will choose to control it. If you were to carry on drinking, after having made an effort to change, then where would the responsibility lie?

To find out a bit more about your attitude to control try asking yourself the following:

If the stress in your life were to suddenly increase for a reason out of your control, how certain are you that you would NOT go back to your old drinking habits?				
very certain	certain	not sure	uncertain	very uncertain
Does your answer to this question trouble you at all or are you happy with it? How about this question? *If someone encouraged you to drink when you are trying to abstain or encouraged you to drink more than you had planned, how easily could you resist?*				
very easily	probably	with difficulty (just about)		couldn't resist

Figure 29   Attitudes to Control

If you think that you might find it difficult to keep to your plan under these circumstances then perhaps alcohol has got quite a hold on you. Ask yourself these questions:

Do you think your use of alcohol is or has been out of control?

Does the prospect of not drinking make you anxious or worried?

Are you worried about your use of alcohol?

Do you find it difficult to stop or go without alcohol?

If you are not certain that you can manage your drinking then you could usefully start to do some work to strengthen your ability to resist and keep to your resolve. This is what the final section of the book is about.

But maybe you are riding high at the moment and are full of confidence that you can keep to your plans. Experience shows though that relapse prevention and relapse planning (more about this later) are still very important to keep things going well. And if things are going badly go over some of the sections from the previous chapters in the book or do some of the sections you may have left out before.

Shortly, we will come to the section of this book called 'keeping on track'. In the alcohol treatment literature the material we are about to cover is known as *relapse prevention*. In the stages of change model (see chapter 3) it is called *maintenance*. It is about helping you to develop a healthy (or at least a healthier) relationship with drinking alcohol for the rest of your life.

Why Bother with the 'Keeping on Track' Phase?

Controlling alcohol doesn't happen by magic; you have to use all your skill, all your resolve and make lots of important decisions. And it really helps if you continue to practice these things regularly. It's hard to change your drinking and it can be even harder to stay changed. Is this a surprise? Did you think it would be easier than this?

If things aren't going too well it can be useful to ask yourself some questions about what is happening. Is your drinking actually out of control or is it just taking a while to establish some new drinking patterns? If you find that you are drinking more than your target it can be helpful to ask yourself 'am I having a lapse or a relapse?'.

Lapses Are Normal — It's What to Expect

A single lapse (drinking more than you had planned to do on a single occasion), does not necessarily need to become a 'relapse' (regular and harmful use of alcohol). It is often possible to catch yourself and take corrective action. We will cover this in much more detail in the next section but here is a quick preview.

Lapses need not become relapses if you:

1. Understand that lapses are likely to occur and recognise them when they do
2. Don't blame yourself or treat the lapse as an unforgivable failure, and

3. Take immediate steps to keep the lapse from happening again (e.g., removing the temptation, getting away from the stress, etc.).

One final thing before moving on: take a moment to reflect on where you have got to so far. If you have made some progress then you should make sure that you reward yourself. It is important to encourage yourself along the way. Even if your progress has been small you can still give yourself some praise. The main thing is to keep going in a positive direction, even if progress is slow and erratic. Remember, developing control over your alcohol use is a journey — but that doesn't mean it has to be a race! Learning to praise yourself for progress can be hard; it is usually easier to criticise yourself, but it is better to be positive. For example, if you kept to your goals for five days out of seven rather than all seven it is still something to be positive about. You should choose your rewards carefully and ensure that you have them straight away (and not wait). But if you are struggling then check that the goals you have chosen suit you.

By the time you have reached this stage of the book, you have probably learned quite a lot about your drinking habits. Do the goals you set for yourself earlier on still suit you? Have you been realistic, over ambitious or too cautious? Everyone who reads this book will be different. Some people are better suited to controlled drinking while others are better off if they cut out alcohol altogether. Are you someone who it will suit to stay abstinent for a while and then slowly go back to drinking, but in a controlled way? Or are you someone who really needs to just stop drinking once and for all? This might be a good time to take stock and think again about what is best for you, right now, in your particular circumstances.

And it might also be a good time to recommit. You started reading this book with some ideas about your drinking and perhaps some intentions to make changes. Are these ideas still up to date? You can use the CLaSS idea as a reminder or checklist for yourself. Here is a reminder: **Communicate** with someone — let them know what you are doing and see if they can encourage you; **Limit** how much you drink (that means having a detailed plan); **Switch** drinks; and **Slow** down.

PART 3

Keeping on Track

CHAPTER 8

Getting a Handle on Things

If you have made a real change to your drinking — fantastic! If you feel that the changes you have made so far are a bit fragile then that is also fantastic, because you realise there is still serious work to do. This is the stage when people work to prevent relapse and consolidate the gains they have made. There is no right time to start this kind of work, but it tends to really get going a few months after having changed your drinking to a safer level and it continues for an indeterminate period after. It's about lasting behaviour change, a new attitude, a new outlook, and a new lifestyle in order to stay in control.

If you're happy with your new approach to drinking, then it will be a lot easier to stay away from heavy drinking. On the other hand, if all you do is change your drinking without making any other changes in your lifestyle and thinking, then you're more likely to slip back into old patterns. In chapter 3 we introduced the stages of change model and now is the time when really understanding that model can be very helpful. If you are not sure you can remember it, or you skipped it earlier, then perhaps you should go back and take a look at that section and the diagram.

As you work through the various stages of the model, you will see that they are arranged in a circle and that there is a direct arrow that goes from 'maintaining change' to 'relapsing'. So, importantly, relapse is part of the cycle. This means that if things don't go exactly according to plan and you have a lapse it doesn't mean that you have failed — it is simply part of the process of learning to control your drinking. If you do have a relapse it is important to be both realistic about why you have had a relapse and also to make sure you don't give yourself too much of a hard time over it. If you mentally beat yourself up you will probably feel down and bad about yourself and then end up drinking more! That's why the relapse box in the diagram points back to the contemplation phase — so you can think about things again. And if you do end up drinking more than you had planned ask yourself this question: 'Am I having a lapse or a relapse?' In other words, is this a 'one off' or is it a repeating pattern? All of these ideas get covered in more detail in the section that follows.

Reasons for Lapses

Rather than blaming yourself for a lapse, have you ever asked why lapses are so common? They are not just something that you may experience, but something that most people go through whenever they try to change a longstanding habit or behaviour. Having the occasional lapse may not be a problem if we know how best to deal with it.

There are many reasons for lapses and it is helpful to understand what they tend to be. But as always it is important to keep in mind that we are thinking about reasons for a relapse and not looking for excuses!

Have a read of the following list of major reasons for a lapse, and consider which of them apply to you. You may recognise one or two apply to you, or many of them, but it would be surprising if none of them rang any bells:

- Not handling negative feelings such as boredom
- Having strong urges or temptations to drink alcohol
- Loneliness
- Difficulty in handling positive feelings
- Anger
- Problems dealing with withdrawal symptoms or health conditions
- Difficulty in handling social pressures to drink
- Testing yourself out to see if your drinking can be controlled
- Not resolving conflicts with others
- Not keeping life in balance (not eating well, not sleeping regularly, not keeping active, spending too much time at work)

If some of these situations or feelings apply to you, there will be a chance later on to do some work to understand how you can overcome these problems — in the section on 'triggers'. If these situations don't apply to you, it would be useful to make a note about what you think your risky times might be.

When Do Relapses Occur?

Consider the following information about addictions: Approximately two thirds of all relapses for any addiction (alcohol, drugs, gambling, smoking) occur within the first 90 days of making a significant change. The reasons for relapse tend to be the same whether the addiction is to alcohol, drugs or gambling.

During the first 90 days after withdrawing from alcohol (or drugs or gambling) people may experience many different kinds of symptoms. These may be physical or psychological. If you are experiencing significant physical withdrawal symptoms or feel very unwell, you need to see your doctor urgently; these physical symptoms can be dangerous or even fatal if not managed appropriately.

Mostly, people think this applies only to people who are actually addicted to alcohol or dependent on it. But it can also apply to those who are heavy or hazardous users (the people this book is mostly aimed at).

During these early days of a reduction in drinking, periods of poor memory or concentration are common. Also, many people find that they overreact to stress. These kinds of reactions may contribute to relapse. The longer a person is abstinent, or is successfully controlling their alcohol intake, the better these things will get; but handling stress is an important way to prevent relapse. Not coping with stress is a major reason for relapse.

Recognise the Danger Signals

A return to alcohol does not just happen out of the blue (even if it seems that way). There is usually a process that leads to the return. But it might not be that obvious what the process is so you have to work out what is going on.

Consider the following: These are some of the danger signals that you can learn to identify. Which of the list below applies to you?

- You begin to isolate yourself from other people and feel bored or lonely much of the time
- You try to impose your way of drinking on other people
- You find yourself easily irritated and relationships become strained
- You doubt your ability to stick to your goals
- Your eating and sleeping patterns are disturbed and you cannot get things done
- You cover up your feelings of unhappiness and hopelessness
- You act impulsively under stress which causes even more stress
- You frequently feel sorry for yourself
- You think you will never have problems with alcohol again so you reject offers of help and don't read books like this one
- You think you can handle alcohol now and it will help you to feel more at ease.

Triggers

Is there anything that sets you off? This is a very important question. If there are particular situations, people, places or feelings that mean you are more likely to drink or drink more than you intend to drink, then you need to know about them. In chapter 2 we introduced the suggestion of keeping a drinking diary. If you have done this then this is the point when it can be a very useful tool. Look back and see what your triggers are — a lot of the information that you need will be there. Your 'drink more' triggers will stand out; but what about your 'drink less' triggers? Can you also pick out the people you never drink with, the situations when you have no difficulty controlling your intake or the feelings you have when you hardly ever want a drink? It is worth making a list of these as well, as this may be very useful in helping you to keep a handle on your drinking.

With this information to hand, the obvious tactic is to avoid your 'drink more' triggers and spend more time in your 'drink less' situations — only life isn't that simple, of course. No matter how determined, well organised or just plain lucky you are, it is almost certain that there will be times when you end up in a 'drink more' situation and can't manoeuvre yourself into a 'drink less' one. In these circumstances you need to be able to deal with these triggers and overcome the habitual tendency to drink more than you planned to. This is what 'thinking about drinking' is all about. A 'thinker drinker' is someone who is aware of their triggers and is able to choose to do something different. So instead of reacting to a 'drink more' trigger by drinking, he or she recognises what his or her usual reaction would have been and decides to respond differently this time, choosing to do something else instead.

There are likely to be some particularly high-risk situations in which you are at more risk than others. Examples might be:

- Passing by a bar where I used to drink heavily
- When I am with others who are drinking
- When I think nobody really cares about me
- When I have to meet people I don't know
- When I am feeling down about problems at home or at work
- When I feel I am being punished unjustly
- When I feel afraid
- When I am on holidays
- When I feel particularly happy and things are going well
- When I have money to spend
- When I remember the good times when I was drinking
- When I experience hassles and arguments
- When I feel resentful
- When I feel irritable or tired
- When there is something to celebrate
- When I am feeling sorry for myself
- When I feel I deserve a drink
- When I am hungry or thirsty
- When I start thinking I don't have a problem with alcohol
- When I find myself getting angry
- When it is a birthday or Christmas
- When I start feeling frustrated or fed up with life
- When I feel disappointed that other people are letting me down
- When I strongly disagree with someone
- When I feel lonely or bored
- When I feel pressured by debt or lack of money

There will no doubt be other examples that you think of. Make a list of the ones that apply to you and then write down what you can do in each one of these situations to stop yourself losing control of the situation. You could put the information into a chart like this:

Trigger	Behaviour	Consequence (what I did)
You were nervous and upset	I drank alcohol	I felt calmer for a while
It was 8.00 pm	I drank alcohol	I had fun in the pub
You were going to a party	I drank alcohol	I talked freely to people
You had to make a sale	I drank alcohol	I was successful

Figure 30   Triggers and Behaviour

This chart shows how 'drink more' situations trigger a response (drinking), which has a consequence. It is easy to see in these examples that there appear to be some short-term benefits from having a drink. These short-term benefits encourage drinking and you will need to find other and better ways to manage them than always having a drink.

So now that you know what these high risk situations might be, you are in a position to plan ahead if you think you might be heading towards one of them.
Here is an example: You are at a party with friends and there is a lot of alcohol around. You want to relax and enjoy yourself, but you do not want to drink, or you do not want to drink very much. With a relapse prevention plan, you might bring a non-alcoholic or low-alcoholic drink with you to avoid being pressed to drink alcohol. But if you are not that well organised or caught by surprise you could have answers ready such as:

No thanks, I don't drink anymore.
No thanks, I'm driving.
No thanks, I'm on a diet.
No thanks, I drink too much these days
No thanks, I've got an early start tomorrow morning
No thanks, I'm on medication
No thanks, it makes me sick
No thanks I'm training

If you are with somebody, agree beforehand that you will leave if you feel uncomfortable. And if you are in a risky situation, it is useful to have prepared in advance at least three ways to handle things. If one of these does not work you then have other options to try. There is no need to give up and practising what you will do or say in advance may help. If you have practiced you will be better prepared and then you will be less likely to worry about what to do under pressure. You can stay confident and in control.

Cravings

It is important to look at this topic because it is a concern that affects many people when they consider reducing their alcohol consumption. They may understand that they are not actually physically addicted to alcohol, but they worry that they may experience an urge to drink that they cannot control. This is part of the feeling they have that alcohol controls them rather that the other way around. A common belief is that cravings for alcohol are always physical. And they can be — especially if you are in the withdrawal phase following alcoholic intoxication or alcohol dependence. If you are feeling ill then we strongly advise that you urgently seek medical advice. However, there are also very important psychological factors involved with cravings. We can divide them into three headings:

- **Old Drinking Habits**
- **Alcohol Expectations**
- **Mood, Thinking and Memory**

Old Drinking Habits

Many people who drink heavily have some regular drinking habits. They may drink at the same time, in the same place, with the same people and drink the same alcoholic drink. Imagine that you end up back in one of these old situations — it is highly likely that you will experience a strong feeling that you want to have a drink. If the feeling is really strong it can become a craving. In this state you may feel anxious or uncomfortable — thoughts and images of alcohol fill the mind, it's difficult to concentrate and you keep thinking about how wonderful it would be to have a drink. You may even convince yourself that it would OK to have just the one drink and then you'd stop.

These feelings are very real and they come about for complex reasons. In part they are the product of a learned or conditioned response. This means that when you are back in one of the old drinking situations the body and the mind automatically (and involuntarily) produce these feelings. The craving feels like it's out of your control.

Another way to think about craving is that it is the memory your body has for the effects of drinking. When you are back in one of your old drinking situations your body responds as if it has just started drinking. This is when the psychological part kicks in. These feelings are recognised and identified as enjoyable and are a direct result of the effects of alcohol. The mind then decides that this is a craving for alcohol.

Alcohol Expectations

It's not just how much you drink, it's also what you think about drink. These thoughts are your expectations — the beliefs you have about the effects you are likely to experience from drinking. They are your beliefs about how the consumption of alcohol will affect your emotions, your abilities and your behaviours. This is where society comes in as well. If people generally believe that intoxication leads to aggression, sexual behaviour or rowdy behaviour, then they tend to act that way when they have had a bit to drink. If the belief is that intoxication leads to relaxation and tranquil behaviour, it virtually always leads to those outcomes. So the messages about alcohol that we pick up through the papers, TV programmes, films and our family and friends are incredibly important. They influence what affect we expect alcohol to have on us; and our expectations influence the affect alcohol actually does have on us. It is almost, but not exactly, as if we are following a set of instructions of what it feels like to be drunk (or tipsy if we prefer).

These expectations have an effect and can they have an effect even when we haven't actually had a drink. Psychologists have done research that shows that if you give people a drink and tell them there is alcohol in the drink, they will behave as if they have had a drink even when they haven't. A typical experiment worked something like this. A group of young adults were given glasses with drinks in. The drinks all had very strong peppermint oil added, so it was not possible to tell whether the drink actually contained alcohol or not. Half of the drinks contained alcohol and half didn't. Half of the participants were given the drinks with the alcohol and half were given the drinks without the alcohol. The final twist in this experiment was that half of the participants were given accurate information about what they were drinking and half of them were told the opposite (that they were drinking alcohol when they were not or they were not drinking alcohol when they were). The participants were then allowed to have as many drinks as they wanted and then the experimenters asked them a load of questions and ran some tests. This type of experiment (which psychologists do a lot) is called the 'balanced placebo design'. The results were that people who believed there was alcohol in the drink drank more, whether there actually was alcohol in their drink or not. This group also reported feeling more intoxicated and had slower reaction times.

Expectations about the effects of alcohol are really important. If you believe that drinking makes you more confident, it might well have that effect. If you think it makes you more relaxed, more creative or more sexy then it might do that as well. But remember that alcohol does tend to loosen people's inhibitions. If you choose to drink to give you the courage to say things that you would otherwise keep to yourself, then you might say more than you bargained for and live to regret it!

So what do you believe about the effects that alcohol has on you? Do you believe it changes your behaviour, do you think you notice the effects very quickly, do you consider yourself to be a 'lightweight' or a 'heavyweight' drinker? And do you think that if you have taste of alcohol then you will automatically and inevitably experience a craving for more alcohol?

Mood, Thinking and Memory

Alcohol usually exaggerates mood. People who are feeling miserable when they drink usually get more miserable; and people who are in a good humour when they drink usually feel happier.

Alcohol interferes with thinking. It makes it harder to concentrate and, in particular, it is harder to plan ahead. So once heavy drinking has started, it is harder to stop. Many people who have a history of heavy drinking may have been doing so for years and are on a kind of automatic pilot. Their drinking is unthinking. For example, they always seem to have a glass of wine in their hands and don't notice how much they have consumed. Such people don't think they are drinking, because they don't think *when* they are drinking.

Alcohol also distorts memory. Long-term heavy drinking has very severe effects on memory, particularly short-term memory. So after a few glasses, problem drinkers have great difficulty recalling how much they have drunk.

If you put all this together, you can see why people experience cravings and strong urges to drink. Cravings come about through old habits, expectations about the effects of alcohol, changing moods, poor concentration and poor memory. And this means that cravings are not inevitable. They are the understandable effects of all these different things and they can be changed. There is an old saying in Alcoholics Anonymous: 'one drink — a drunk'. AA does, of course, have an important point. Sometimes the taste of alcohol can trigger such a strong craving for more that it is difficult not to go on drinking. And for these people it is best to avoid tasting alcohol at all. But this is not true for everyone and, if you recognise that craving is often a psychological thing and not a purely physical one, then you can learn to deal with cravings and stay in control. But sometimes you might not be able to manage to stay totally in control. This is what the next section is about.

What About When You Drink More Than You Planned?

Can you imagine a situation when you drank more than you planned? Perhaps you had planned to have just one glass of wine, but finished the bottle. Or maybe you planned just one drink in the pub on the way home, but stayed the whole evening. This is a common experience and can be a problem for people who are trying to control their alcohol use. If this happens (or has happened to you) then it is worthwhile examining the kinds of thoughts you may have had in this situation. Perhaps you had planned to be abstinent or very controlled and then you lapsed and had more than you had intended. If so, did you think any of the following?

- I have been a real idiot — and idiots drink — so I may as well carry on drinking.
- I have blown it now — so I might as well carry on.
- I'll start again tomorrow so I'll enjoy a few drinks now.
- Typical me — I can't get anything right so there is no point in even trying to stop now.
- The alcohol has beaten me again, my self control has gone — so what the hell!

No doubt you can think of your own versions of these thoughts that have passed through your mind.

This pattern of behaviour and thinking has been called the *abstinence violation effect*. These are grand words for quite a straightforward idea. It means, in other words, that if you planned to be abstinent (or controlled) and you drink more than you had planned, then you may go on to break your limit altogether and drink a great deal of alcohol. There are two ways to tackle this problem. You can review your drinking targets to see if you have you set unrealistic or too strict or rigid goals for yourself. Or you can develop more helpful thoughts about what to do when you drink too much and that is what we will concentrate on now.

Controlling the Urge to Drink

Many people trying to control their alcohol use say that they derive no pleasure from their drinking. They say they drink only because of the craving that never seems to stop. Coping with these urges can be exhausting as the urges dominate thinking and greatly interfere with everyday life and daily routines. Many people even feel that they will never function without alcohol, as the urge to drink they experience interferes too much with quality of life.

We cannot expect urges to vanish completely. What can be hoped for is that the urges will become less frequent and that they don't lead to relapse. At times, however, the craving can seem excruciating. You can't get your mind off alcohol, everything you see reminds you of it. You may feel frustrated and have thoughts such as 'I can't stand this!' or 'there is no way I will be able to live without giving in' or 'I'll just go crazy!'.

Thoughts like this, although understandable, can make things seem worse than they are. If you believe that you are completely out of control, your emotions will follow. What is important to remember is that urges are normal and typically reduce as you make changes in your drinking habits.

You should try not to think in black and white terms using words like 'horrible' or 'unbearable'. Belief in horrible extremes only makes you feel worse. When you think like this you can get a bit disconnected from ordinary thinking. In reality, ask yourself just how unbearable is your urge actually right now. Is it as unbearable as, for example, getting stabbed in the stomach? Or better still, what have you endured which was worse than your current urge? Was that unbearable? If so, does it follow that your urge to drink is less than unbearable and perhaps really only just very uncomfortable.

Distraction

Some urges are so relentless that talking back to them is insufficient. You still can't get your mind off your habit. You may need to try distracting yourself. You could try some form of mental exercise or an activity. For example, you could use an image to take your mind off an urge which is dominating your mind. Conjuring up a pleasant place like a beach or on a raft in a lake can help you to take your mind off the urge and relax as well.

However, relaxing images are not helpful for everyone. Instead, you could find some mental task that will be very difficult to finish, but which is interesting and consuming, that you can activate in response to an urge. You could try planning the perfect holiday, creating the ideal money-making business, recalling a dream from the night before or maybe attempting a difficult quiz, crossword or Sudoku puzzle. You could have some games on your phone that you specially reserve for when the urge to drink is really strong. If the urge is really intense, you could try identifying everything in the room that is blue or naming as many objects within eyesight that begin with the letter N. These ideas may sound crazy but they can help a bit and are worth a try.

Staying with the Feeling

Sometimes the opposite to distraction may work even better. Instead of psychologically moving away from the urge to drink, the aim is to stay with the feeling until it gets less intense. Generally speaking, if you can resist the urge to drink for about 15 minutes, then the urge becomes less intense and sometimes goes away altogether (until the next time). This approach is called *exposure therapy* and is sometimes used as part of alcohol treatment programmes. It can help you to get confident, because even when you feel the urge to drink and crave alcohol, you have some experience of resisting the urge and of not drinking.

You can also try *urge surfing*. This is not an extreme sport or a new computer game. It's the idea that when an urge comes you don't try to change or stop the feeling, but just allow yourself to go along with it. Just like surfing on the sea, eventually the wave dies away and you are left with calm, still water.

Dealing with Temptation

Let's face it, most people drink because they like it — it's just that some people like it more than is good for them (and others) and they can't stop when they want to or feel they should. But temptation is something we deal with all the time in different ways. We might be tempted to eat chocolate, steal from a shop, tell a lie, have an affair, cheat in an exam — the list is endless — and (mostly) we resist the temptation and don't do it. So we can apply the lessons we have learned in dealing with these examples of temptation to deal with the temptation to drink.

Start by thinking of an example of when you have stopped doing something you like doing because it wasn't good for you or somebody else (it doesn't have to be a big thing). Now describe the situation to yourself in detail and then go on to describe how you managed to achieve the success in stopping (even if it was only a little or brief success). For example you may have stopped eating chips, biting your finger nails or over spending on credit cards. How did you achieve this? Was it just will power, did you get help from anyone or did you make use of some particular techniques? If you can recognise what you did in those situations, then you can apply this learning to drinking situations. Realising that you do have the capacity to deal with temptation sometimes is confidence boosting and that is what is needed to deal with the temptation to drink.

'I Didn't Mean to Have a Drink but…'

Sometimes it seems that despite our best plans we just sort of end up in situations where drinking is more likely to happen. Is this really true or is there something else at work here? Psychologists have noticed that these situations may seem to come out of the blue but they actually develop out of lots of little steps and choices. On their own, these steps seem tiny or unimportant, but taken together they have an undesired result. They are called 'seemingly irrelevant decisions'.

Here is an example. Imagine people who are trying to reduce their drinking who might think that they just 'ended up in the pub'; but, on closer inspection, they can see that it wasn't an accident at all. There were probably lots of little decisions that they had made before they took their first drink, decisions which pushed them closer and closer to drinking. They may, for example, have had a tough day at work and decided to take a route home which just happened to pass through the area where they used to live. Then they bumped in to an old friend, then they wanted to catch up on some gossip and without thinking about it they are in the pub having a quick drink which then leads on to a long drinking session. And on the morning after, there are lots of regrets and they can't 'quite work out how it happened'.

Or imagine stopping off to get some shopping at the supermarket on the way home from work. You decide that you would like to cook something fancy for dinner. Rather than going straight to the till, you find yourself strolling up and down the aisles, looking for a non-alcoholic drink to go with the meal, but you can't find anything you want. You decide to call a friend and invite them over. You are vaguely aware that this friend drinks quite a lot and would expect to have wine with the meal, but you dismiss this concern and think that you don't need to worry because you feel sure that you won't have a drink on a weekday evening. The friend readily agrees to come over and offers to bring a bottle. Then you think it would be mean if you didn't have some wine to offer as well. Within moments your footsteps have taken you to the wine section (cunningly situated, by the supermarket designers, next to the non-alcoholic drinks). That evening, you end up sharing two bottles of wine over dinner with your friend.

These moment to moment choices — the seemingly irrelevant decisions — are all those choices, rationalisations, and minimisations of risk that move people closer to, or even into, high-risk situations; although each step may seem to be unrelated to drinking at the time. In other words, people underestimate the likelihood that they will be tempted to drink and overestimate their ability to resist. But this all happens very quickly, and we don't realise the importance of each decision at the time.

Interrupting one of these chains of decisions is easier at the beginning than at the end. It is, for example, much easier to go straight home after a heavy day at work and not have a drink than if you have actually gone to the pub, bar, or restaurant. The problem is that the decisions at the beginning of the chain are trickier to spot than the ones later down the line.

It is amazing how much self-deception we are capable of. We can tell ourselves, for example, that the route past the pub is the quickest (when it isn't), or that we are doing a friend a favour by accompanying them to the pub. A common self-deception is the idea that 'I've got to have some drink in the house for guests'. Did you notice the 'got to' — this is always a danger signal. In fact, there is no obligation to have drink in the house; actually, it's a choice.

Making a Lapse Management Plan

What happens if you do have a lapse? It doesn't need to be a disaster. You need ways to turn things around quickly so that you can get back on course. To do this, it's best to plan how you are going to manage in advance, before the lapse happens. Hopefully, you will never need to put this plan into action, but you should have it ready. Just like carrying an umbrella around with you, it is best if you have the umbrella with you when it rains, rather than having to go and fetch or buy one when it has started pouring.

You will need to do some advance thinking to get your plan into shape, and it will be best if you type it out so you can carry it around with you. Print it onto a piece of paper (or card is better) and keep it in your pocket or bag. Or have it as a document stored on your computer or as a note or reminder on your phone. There is an example of a plan below.

My lapse Management plan (or what I would do if I slip up)

If I slip up I could:

Phone or text a friend

Write the name of your friend here with their phone number

Read the notes I have made doing the exercises in this book

Leave the situation where I am drinking

Do something I enjoy (not alcohol related)

Take some exercise

Remind yourself of your original reasons for changing your drinking

Other ideas

Figure 31   Lapse Management Plan Example

No doubt you will be able to think of lots of your own ideas to put into your lapse management plan. The exercises in the earlier parts of this book, the information from your drinking diary, understanding your own 'drink more' and 'drink less' triggers and reminding yourself of the original reasons you started this process will all help you. It is up to you to stop a lapse becoming a relapse or, worse still, a collapse. Being gentle and firm will probably work better than frightening or condemning yourself.

CHAPTER 9

Building a Balanced Lifestyle

Many people who are (or who have been) heavy drinkers notice that their alcohol use has distorted their lifestyle. Much of their time has been structured around regular drinking and it is really helpful to change this. They may find that they have used alcohol to cope with problems and to regulate their mood. This kind of relationship with alcohol is not at all healthy. To be able to adopt more positive behaviour around drinking you may need find ways to fill the gap that alcohol used to fill. However, it's not easy — old habits die hard and it needs some careful thinking about and planning. In this chapter we will help you to build a more balanced lifestyle. The topics covered in this chapter will also help you to build resilience, so that you are better able to cope with some of the hard things that life may throw at you. In this chapter we will cover:

- Finding new ways to spend your time
- Coping with fears and anxieties
- Relaxation
- Assertiveness
- Sleep
- Nutrition
- Relationships

Finding New Ways to Spend Your Time

When drinking is regular and heavy it is often the case that people's lifestyles become more and more focused on alcohol. Quite often they find themselves thinking about alcohol a lot and notice that they tend to drink in the same places and at the same times and with the same people. There is little time left for anything else. One result is that they don't do other things that they might enjoy or that make them feel good. Often they find that they have given up on favourite activities and they don't use skills and abilities that they have. As a result, people sometimes feel bored, aimless and don't feel good about themselves.

A common example of this, which might apply to your own life, is sport. Perhaps in the past you were a good swimmer, footballer or runner. Maybe you used to go to the gym regularly, but, as alcohol featured more in your life, you found yourself going less. It may feel daunting to go back (perhaps you worry that you won't be as good as you used to be) so it is time for a new approach and to develop some more options and choices for yourself.

Early on in this book you were encouraged to look at some of the things you have stopped doing because of your drinking. You might want to go back and look at those sections again. It can be helpful to make a list of things you used to enjoy doing and see what it is that you have dropped. If you are short of ideas then take a look at the list in figure 32. Most of them are serious suggestions, although one or two are a bit tongue-in-cheek.

If you reflect on this list, you might find things that you want to take up or start doing again. But if there is nothing here to inspire you then you can produce some more ideas by brainstorming. Brainstorming is a way of creatively generating lots of new ideas. It works better if you can do this with a group of people, but is useful to do on your own as well. Get a piece of paper and write your question on the top. The question should be something like 'what activities can I do to fill my time instead of drinking?' You can modify this if you can think of a better question. Start writing down as many ideas as you can. The key thing is not to edit as you go along — the more ideas the better and it doesn't matter if they are a bit unusual or even if they sound crazy! At this stage, you don't have to do them you just have to think of them. There are four main principles to follow when brainstorming:

1. Focus on quantity because the more ideas you have the better the quality of the ideas you have overall;
2. Withhold criticism and if you are not sure about something you have written down don't judge it but put your doubts 'on hold' for the moment;
3. Welcome unusual ideas because to get a good and long list of unusual ideas helps;
4. Combine and improve the ideas by associating one with another.

When you have a long list of ideas, you can start to edit and think about which ones you could actually do. Possibilities might be:

Things I can do alone.

Things that are free.

Things I have always wanted to do but never dared.

Places I always said I'd go to.

People I know by sight but have never talked to.

Having these ideas and plans is great, but there is another step involved in making them actually happen in a regular and useful way. It means getting down to the detail and committing yourself. The exercise in figure 33 might help; you could try it every day for a week or more often if it is useful. If you are working or doing some kind of regular activity then you might not need to put in all the details. Instead, just fill it in where there are gaps in your weekly schedule, such as evenings, weekends or holidays.

Which of these have you done or noticed recently?

Soaking in the Bath	☐	Having family get-togethers	☐
Repairing things around the house (DIY)	☐	Reading magazines or newspapers	☐
Collecting things (coins, shells, etc.)	☐	Going for a drive / bike ride	☐
Working on my car / motorbike	☐	Sex	☐
Having quiet evenings	☐	Spending an evening with good friends	☐
Relaxing	☐	Planning a day's activities	☐
Going to the cinema	☐	Meeting new people	☐
Watching a video or DVD	☐	Singing around the house	☐
Going swimming, jogging or walking	☐	Saving money	☐
Thinking I have done a full day's work	☐	Practicing religion (going to church, praying, etc.)	☐
Exercising	☐	Losing weight	☐
Listening to music	☐	Cooking and/or eating nice food	☐
Buying household gadgets	☐	Thinking I'm an OK person	☐
Laughing	☐	A day with nothing to do	☐
Listening to others	☐	Sightseeing	☐
Going fishing	☐	Gardening	☐

Playing with animals	☐		
Buying things for myself (perfume, golf balls, etc.)	☐		
Talking on the phone	☐		
Sending emails	☐		
Going to museums	☐		
Being alone	☐		
Lighting candles	☐		
Writing diary entries or letters	☐		
Listening to the radio	☐		
Cleaning	☐		
Saying "I love you"	☐		
Taking children places	☐		
Thinking about my good qualities	☐		
Dancing	☐		
Buying books	☐		
Going on a picnic	☐		

Figure 32   Recent Activities Questionnaire (*Continued*)

☐	Working	☐	Going skating	☐	Having a sauna
☐	Thinking about pleasant events	☐	Going to the hairdressers or beauticians	☐	Thinking "I did that pretty well" after doing something
☐	Discussing books	☐	Playing tennis	☐	Meditating
☐	Making / buying a gift for someone	☐	Painting	☐	Going boating
☐	Watching sport	☐	Kissing	☐	Having lunch with a friend
☐	Travelling to national parks	☐	Doing something spontaneous	☐	Fantasising about the future
☐	Completing a task	☐	Thinking I have a lot more going for me than most people	☐	Sitting in a café
☐	Buying clothes	☐	Sleeping	☐	Playing cards
☐	Doing puzzles (jigsaw, crossword, Sudoku)	☐	Going to plays and concerts	☐	Working out in the gym
☐	Surfing the web	☐	Daydreaming	☐	Having a political discussion
☐	Photography	☐	Entertaining	☐	Thinking about becoming active in the community
☐	Thinking I'm a person who can cope	☐	Thinking about sex	☐	Watching clouds
☐	Sending a text	☐	Flirting	☐	Doing something new
☐	Playing pool	☐	Doing arts and crafts	☐	Playing an instrument
☐	Dressing up and looking nice	☐	Going out to dinner	☐	Reflecting on how I've improved

Figure 32　Recent Activities Questionnaire

Today's date 21/04/2012	Fill out the night before what you plan to do	Fill out at the end of the day what you actually did
Early Morning (Wake-up until 10 am)		
Late Morning (10 am-12 pm)		
Early Afternoon (12 pm-3 pm)		
Late Afternoon (3 pm-5 pm)		
Evening (5pm-8pm)		
Night (8pm until bed)		

Figure 33   Worksheet of Planned and Actual Daily Activities

DIRECTIONS: In the first column, plan what you want to do tomorrow. Then, tomorrow night, fill out the next column with the details of what you actually did.

Having an activity plan can be very helpful. You can begin to see the gaps in your day and in your week where drinking might slip in and you can plan something to help fill those times.

Coping with Fears and Anxieties

There are many reasons why people lose control of their drinking. One common reason is that people have anxieties and fears that they have not been able to deal with in other ways. Many people use alcohol to give themselves 'Dutch courage' and without it they don't feel capable of carry on some of the activities they want to do.

If anxiety and stress are a significant problem for you, then you would be well advised to seek help to learn how to manage and deal with it. It is beyond the scope of this book to deal with stress management techniques in detail. There are a lot of helpful kinds of therapy for anxiety disorders. In particular, cognitive behavioural therapy has been developed to treat the whole range of serious anxieties that people have (such as panic, social phobia, obsessive compulsive disorder, post traumatic stress disorder, worry). However, we can give a few ideas on one way of learning to get through stressful situations. One technique is to imagine what it is going to be like before you actually have to do it and to learn to relax your way through. This is done by imagining it in steps starting with the least stressful and getting relaxed about that before moving on. (There are instructions for relaxation below in the relaxation section.)

Here is an example. Stephanie did not like going to parties and if she were going to one then she would drink quite a bit beforehand. To help her get over this problem she made a list of all the things that were involved in going to a party starting with the least stressful:

1. Lying in the bath
2. Getting Dressed
3. Putting on make up
4. Putting on her coat
5. Leaving her own home
6. Ringing the doorbell
7. Entering the room
8. Talking to someone she doesn't already know
9. Saying the wrong thing

After writing down this list, Stephanie relaxed completely using some relaxation techniques that we will come to in the next section. She then tried to imagine herself doing the first item on her list, 'lying in the bath'. She tried to make it as vivid as possible. If it frightened her she went back to relaxing. Then she tried again.

Once she could relax for 30 seconds thinking about 'lying in the bath' she went on to number 2. And so on until she could manage number 8 and even number 9. This was just the beginning of learning to deal with this problem and there are a lot more steps involved in overcoming it. It may be that Stephanie's problem was quite significant and she could have had social phobia. If so, she would probably get some benefit from a course of cognitive behaviour therapy. However, sometimes people have got out of the habit of doing things they once found a bit difficult and some simple techniques can be quite helpful in getting started again. One useful technique is relaxation training.

Relaxation

Many people say they drink in order to relax. They drink when they feel tense and the alcohol helps them to unwind. So it makes sense to find other ways to relax. Finding relaxing activities is very helpful, but there are also specific relaxation techniques that you can learn. The technique below is called *progressive muscle relaxation*. It is quite easy to buy recordings of the instructions teaching the technique if you wish. They can be downloaded on line and you can often find CDs in health food stores. To get the benefits you will need to practice regularly — certainly at least once a day for quite a while. If you don't have access to a recording (or don't like the recording you have) then you make your own recording and use your own voice to guide you through the instructions.

	Instructions
Step 1 (Feet)	Settle yourself comfortably and then very slowly tense both feet as hard as you can. Hold them like that for a few seconds, and then relax. Do it again.
Step 2 (Legs)	Tense your legs in the same way. (Don't worry if your feet and face and hands tense up as well, they probably will) This time as you relax, breathe out hard — you'll find it helps you to relax more quickly and more deeply. Do it again.
Step 3 (Back)	Slowly . . . work through the rest of your body in exactly the same way . . . . . . tensing and relaxing your back muscles. Do it again
Step 4 (Tummy)	Slowly . . . work through the rest of your body in exactly the same way . . . . . . tensing and relaxing your tummy muscles. Do it again
Step 5 (Hands)	Slowly . . . work through the rest of your body in exactly the same way . . . . . . tensing and relaxing your hands. Do it again
Step 6 (Arms)	Slowly . . . work through the rest of your body in exactly the same way . . . . . . tensing and relaxing your arms. Do it again
Step 7 (Chest)	Slowly . . . work through the rest of your body in exactly the same way . . . . . . tensing and relaxing your chest. Do it again
Step 8 (Shoulders)	Slowly . . . work through the rest of your body in exactly the same way . . . . . . tensing and relaxing your shoulders. Do it again.

Figure 34   Relaxation Instructions

Unwinding — Things to Remember

Don't forget to breathe out every time you relax.

Instead of tensing your neck muscles, get rid of stiffness by rolling your head slowly and gently from side to side and then forwards and backwards. Feel the muscles stretching and relaxing.

It's often quite difficult to relax your face muscles. Try pulling faces — lower your eyebrows, purse your lips, wrinkle your nose. Stay like this for a few seconds then relax.

Don't forget to breathe out!

Once you're feeling comfortable, take some time to enjoy it. Each time you breathe out, picture tension flowing away so that you relax more and more deeply. Imagine that you are somewhere peaceful and quiet . . . in the country, perhaps, or by the sea.

Don't worry if you find it hard to relax at first — it takes time to learn to do this properly.

Do practice every day.

Don't hurry — you won't relax properly if you rush.

Don't feel guilty about taking the time to do it properly.

Don't despair if you've tried and still can't manage it. You might find it easier with a relaxation tape or CD. Or, you could think about joining a class to learn relaxation.

Assertiveness

Assertiveness is about being more effective. It can be helpful to be assertive in many different situations that you may come across. It is particularly important to be assertive when confronted by a high-risk drinking situation.

We discussed being assertive in drinking situations in chapter 7. For someone who has a history of heavy drinking, being assertive when saying 'no' to a drink is very important. Other people may put you under quite a bit of pressure to drink. It is worthwhile remembering that these people may be heavy drinkers themselves and also are not used to you not drinking or not drinking so much. It is best to be clear with yourself about how much you plan to drink (if anything) and have some good arguments ready in advance.

Assertiveness involves:

• being clear about what you feel, what you need and how it can be achieved
• being able to communicate calmly without attacking another person
• saying 'yes' when you want to, and saying 'no' when you mean no (rather than agreeing to do something just to please someone else)
• deciding on, and sticking to, clear boundaries — being happy to defend your position, even if it provokes conflict
• being confident about handling conflict if it occurs
• understanding how to negotiate if two people want different outcomes
• being able to talk openly about yourself and being able to listen to others
• having confident, open body language
• being able to give and receive positive and negative feedback
• having a positive, optimistic outlook

Body Language

An important part of assertiveness is open, secure body language. The way that you hold yourself has an impact on how you are perceived and treated. Passive body language would be the classic 'victim' stance of hunched shoulders and avoidance of eye contact, while an aggressive stance is one with clenched fists, glaring eyes and intrusive body language. Assertive people generally stand upright but in a relaxed manner, looking people calmly in the eyes, with open hands.

Communication

Clear communication is also an important part of assertiveness. This is where you show knowledge — you are able to understand and summarise the situation and your feelings — you understand what the situation needs and you are able to explain clearly what you want or need, give your reasons and any benefits to the other party. You need a clear head to be able to do this. Alcohol can blur your thinking and your speech.

Alcohol and Sleep

Heavy drinking can play havoc with sleep. As we saw in chapter 4, poor sleep contributes to poor physical and psychological health. In this section we will look at the effects alcohol can have on sleep in more detail. Heavy drinking can have bad effects on the amount you sleep and how well you sleep. If you are not sleeping well, you may be tempted into using alcohol to help you get off to sleep (maybe as a nightcap) and the cycle of heavy drinking is perpetuated. And if you feel tired during the day, then you may not have the concentration and determination to manage your drinking.

The effects of alcohol on sleep are many and varied. It is certainly true that alcohol can help people fall asleep, but this may not always be an advantage. Alcohol is a drug and it interferes drastically with the normal pattern of sleeping. People who go to bed with a significant amount of alcohol in their bloodstream tend to have poor quality sleep as well as a shorter amount of sleep overall. Alcohol can also produce a kind of sleep with no dreams. This is a problem because dreams are very important for emotional and physical wellbeing.

A balanced lifestyle requires regular, deep sleep. This kind of sleep is refreshing and renewing — very different from an alcohol-induced stupor or the restless, dreamless sleep of the frequent heavy drinker. How well do you sleep? Do you have difficulty getting off to sleep? Do you wake up early, sleep lightly or are easily woken? Do you wake up feeling sleepy and not refreshed? If some of these apply to you, then you may need to address your sleep problem and try to find a solution that doesn't involve alcohol. Using alcohol to get you off to sleep can prevent you from learning how to get to sleep naturally. A great deal of insomnia is the result of unhelpful sleeping habits and poor sleeping conditions. There are some useful tips for better sleep without using alcohol or drugs.

Improving Sleep

- Sleep only when sleepy — this reduces the time you are awake in bed. If you can't fall asleep within 20 minutes, get up and do something relaxing until you feel sleepy, sit quietly in the dark and don't expose yourself to bright light while you are up. The light gives cues to your brain that it is time to wake up.
- Don't take naps during the daytime — this will ensure you are tired at bedtime.
- Get up and go to bed the same time every day, even on weekends! When your sleep cycle has a regular rhythm, you will feel better.
- Refrain from exercise at least 4 hours before bedtime. Regular exercise is recommended to help you sleep well, but the timing of the workout is important. Exercising in the morning or early afternoon will not interfere with sleep.
- Develop sleep rituals — it is important to give your body cues that it is time to slow down and sleep. Listen to relaxing music, read something soothing for 15 minutes, have a cup of caffeine-free or herbal tea, do relaxation exercises.
- Only use your bed for sleeping — refrain from using your bed to watch TV, pay bills, do work or reading. So when you go to bed your body knows it is time to sleep. Sex is the only exception.
- Stay away from caffeine, nicotine and alcohol at least 4–6 hours before bed. Caffeine and nicotine are stimulants that interfere with your ability to fall asleep. Coffee, tea, cola, cocoa, chocolate and some prescription and non-prescription drugs contain caffeine. Cigarettes and some drugs contain nicotine.
- Have a light snack before bed — if your stomach is too empty, that can interfere with sleep. However, if you eat a heavy meal before bedtime, that can interfere as well.
- Take a hot bath 90 minutes before bedtime — a hot bath will raise your body temperature, but it is the drop in body temperature after the bath that may leave you feeling sleepy.
- Make sure your bed and bedroom are quiet and comfortable — a hot room can be uncomfortable. A cooler room along with enough blankets to stay warm is recommended. If light in the early morning bothers you, get a blackout shade or wear a slumber mask. If noise bothers you, try earplugs.
- Use sunlight to set your biological clock — as soon as you get up in the morning, go outside and get some sunlight for at least 15 minutes.

Alcohol and Nutrition (We Are What We Eat and Drink)

Heavy drinkers often eat poorly. They may grab food on the run, eat irregularly and rely on alcohol for their calories. We discussed in chapter 4 some of the problems that can be caused by a combination of poor diet and alcohol consumption. To summarise, the supply of essential nutrients is restricted and this affects both energy and the ability of the body to keep itself in good shape. Alcohol itself also interferes with digestion and the storage, use and excretion of nutrients. This can result in obesity, poor general health, stomach problems, liver problems, muscle problems, memory problems, reduced fertility — the list is almost endless. So it's very important to take nutrition and healthy eating seriously.

Many long-term drinkers substitute alcohol for food and become malnourished. They may develop liver disease which often diminishes the appetite. So attention to a good eating pattern is very important. A damaged liver affects the body's ability to absorb and make use of the nourishment in food. Deficiencies of vitamin B often occur in alcoholic liver damage. Recovery from severe liver damage may be helped by improving nutrition, if necessary with supplements prescribed by a doctor. Taking a daily multivitamin tablet (which contains a range of B and other vitamins) may be helpful.

So what steps should I take?

- Sensible eating is the key to good health, so try to avoid living on toast and chips. A poor diet might not make you ill in itself straight away, but it will increase your risk of developing other illnesses. To ensure you have a nutritious diet it is recommended that you include meat and fish or a good vegetarian alternative, fruit and vegetables, food containing fibre and carbohydrates. Try to avoid too much fat, sugar and salt in your diet. It's also important to avoid a lot of caffeine and drink lots of water.
- Alcohol can sometimes suppress appetite. You may not feel like eating when you drink and may not remember to eat properly. It can be helpful to plan regular meals and even eat before having a drink.

Alcohol and Relationships

Heavy drinking can have a very big effect on relationships. This is especially true if you are, or have been, a long-term heavy drinker. There are a lot of ways in which people close to you may become involved in your drinking. For example, some of the people closest to you may also be heavy drinkers. This can make it very difficult keep your own drinking under control. If they are used to seeing you drink, they may end up encouraging you to drink more. It may be a habit or it may be more than that — perhaps they are subtly encouraging you to drink more as a way of justifying their own drinking. It's worth thinking about.

There is an approach to treating people with alcohol problems called *social behaviour and network therapy*. It had a brief mention in chapter 3, but we didn't go into much detail. Here are some exercises from this approach that might be worth having a go at. The basic idea is that you have more chance of sticking to your drinking goals if you are surrounded by other people who will support the changes you want to make.

Make a list of the five or six people you spend time with and then ask yourself 'do they drink?'. When you make this list remember to be as inclusive as you can and include any groups you belong to: work colleagues, family members, friends and neighbours. Could you estimate how much they drink? It may not be obvious and a little unobtrusive research could help (but don't be too invasive or nosy or you could end up alienating them). Do they encourage you to drink? What kind of influence do they have on you? Can you recall any examples of situations when their influence was a problem for you and may have encouraged you to drink to excess?

Completing this kind of exercise can be a little disturbing. It is not easy to admit that your best mate from childhood, your sister, your spouse or your neighbour is having a negative influence. But it is better to be honest and face up to the situation head on than close your eyes and pretend that the problem isn't there.

The next step is to ask yourself what needs to change about your relationship with these people. Is there anything you need to do or say to make things easier for yourself when you are around these people? Or perhaps you would do better by keeping away from them, at least for a while. And if you choose this then you will need some explanations to hand.

In the early days, when you first try to change your drinking habits, you may find that friends, spouses, relatives or work mates can be very helpful and supportive. But after a while, especially if it gets difficult, then, like you, they can get ground down by it and 'burn out'. As a result you may feel depressed and end up withdrawing and spending more time on your own. When you are on your own thoughts can easily end up in a depressive spiral and you think no one wants to spend time with you and you can end up feeling useless. You will need to guard against this and develop a positive approach to improving your relationships

It's a big thing to make a long-term change in your drinking patterns. Hopefully, you will get a positive response from those around you, but if you don't here are some things to think about that may help:

- Reduce expectations of yourself and other people. You cannot expect to feel as loving, close, intimate or sexy when you are doing something this big (at least for a while).
- Don't try to change other people. It will only lead to frustration and the emphasis needs to be on looking after yourself.
- Be fair to yourself and to others. Don't make demands on yourself or on others that are too great. Don't make promises that you can't keep just to keep the peace. This usually doesn't work.
- Don't become isolated or cut yourself off from people who care about you. You might explain what is happening and that right now you cannot be as responsive as you would like to be; but that doesn't mean you don't care. However, if there is someone around who you always find upsetting or argumentative, then it is usually best to avoid them for a while.
- Listen to others and give them time to talk about themselves. This may seem very hard when you are feeling low yourself, but it may pay dividends. People appreciate being listened to and it will also take you out of yourself and will help to break the cycle of thinking about your own problems all the time.

You may also want to consider building a new network of people around you who can support your new approach to alcohol. Some people find organisations such as

Alcoholics Anonymous really helpful and attend meetings regularly (even daily), but AA is definitely not for everyone. Another approach is to develop your own network. Think about who you would find it useful to spend more time with and make arrangements to see them. Making a proper list is the most helpful way to do this. Thinking about the list of people is a good start, but actually writing it down often works better. Make sure you have the phone numbers to hand and if you need to get in touch with an old friend that you haven't seen for a while, this would be a good place to start.

CHAPTER 10

The Research Background

Throughout this book there have been references to research. For the final chapter we thought it might be of interest to briefly describe some of the studies that have formed the basis of the approach. Most of the theories and psychological approaches underpinning the ideas in this book were described in chapter 3. The research we will discuss now are the studies evaluating the effectiveness of these approaches.

Project Match

Any account of research in the alcohol field must include a description of Project Match. It was the biggest, most expensive and most ambitious alcohol treatment research project ever undertaken. Its aims were simple enough: to establish which kinds of alcohol treatment work best and whether some people respond to one type of therapy better than others. The project began in 1989, took eight years to carry out, and many more years to analyse the results. It was funded by the National Institute for Alcohol and Alcoholism (in the USA) and was run in more than nine treatment centres across America. It brought together some of the most well established alcohol treatment researchers in the world.

The three types of therapy were the ones most well known and widely available at the time. These were cognitive behaviour therapy, motivational enhancement therapy (which is similar to motivational interviewing) and the twelve-step programme. The research findings were very confusing and not that helpful. The authors of the research concluded that all three types of treatment were equally effective — they all worked. Other people criticised these conclusions and said that they were all equally ineffective — none of them worked. Matching to type of treatment wasn't that helpful either. After a lot of very sophisticated analysis, the researchers suggested that the twelve-step programme worked best for clients who were 'dependent' and were part of networks of people who were 'pro-drinking'. Motivational enhancement therapy, on the other hand, was better for angry clients. There was some evidence that shorter treatments worked as well as long ones.

United Kingdom Alcohol Treatment Trial (UKATT)

UKATT was less ambitious (and less expensive). There were three treatment centres (Birmingham, Cardiff and Leeds) and researchers allocated people to either motivational interviewing or to a new kind of therapy called social behaviour and network therapy so that their effectiveness could be compared with each other. Both groups reported substantial reductions in alcohol consumption, dependence, drinking related problems and better quality of life. The research included a study of the cost effectiveness of alcohol treatment. They found that that the therapies resulted in substantial savings across health and social services, saving the public purse five times as much per client as the sum spent on their treatment.

Relapse Prevention

The results of research into the effectiveness of the relapse prevention approach have done rather well. Relapse prevention reduces the frequency of relapses after treatment and when relapses do happen they are less intense and don't last as long. People who have used the relapse prevention approach tend not to be totally abstinent from alcohol, but they are likely to drink less overall than those who had a different treatment approach. The benefits tend to show up from about a year after treatment has been completed.

Controlled Drinking

Controlled drinking was developed as an alternative to abstinence for dependent drinkers. This approach has been incredibly valuable and the approach in this book has benefited extensively from the research generated by the treatment model. There have been a number of research studies showing its effectiveness for low to moderate drinkers.

The research into controlled drinking began with the simple observation that there were plenty of people who had once been diagnosed as alcoholic, but were later found to be drinking normally. If alcoholism were a disease and abstinence were the cure, then logically this would not have been possible. Instead of abstinence it proved possible to teach people how to drink in a controlled way. There were a set of skills that could be learned. Dozens of studies have been conducted demonstrating the success of this approach with so-called alcoholics in the clinic settings and 'problem drinkers' in community settings.

The debate appeared to be settled in the mid 1970s and treatment programmes were being rolled out. However, in the early eighties some of the main researchers in the field were accused of falsifying their data. These accusations turned out to be false, but it took a long time before the air was finally cleared. The researchers who had been accused received regular abusive and threatening letters, and it became very difficult for them to obtain funding for their research. It appears that there was a very powerful lobby in favour of the abstinence only approach.

Drug Treatments

The most well known drug treatment is antabuse (disulfiram). This drug works by creating a negative and extremely unpleasant physical reaction when a person drinks alcohol. It tends to be used following a period of detoxification and is only suitable for someone intending not to drink. There are significant risks using this approach and the drug is only available from medical specialists; use and dose must be closely supervised. Unsurprisingly, it only works while someone is using it, so relapse rates are high. If someone takes it for a long period, then they may learn to not drink and then the outcomes are better.

There are drugs available to reduce cravings (in Europe but not so far in the US), but they are not widely available and are still being tested in clinical trials. Also, drugs are used to help control and reduce withdrawal symptoms during detoxification. These medications make detox safe as without them alcohol withdrawal would be more dangerous. Anyone who is dependent and choosing to withdraw from alcohol use needs medical advice and support.

Alcohol use can sometimes coexist with psychological disorders such as depression. Antidepressants are not a treatment for alcohol problems themselves and it is recommended that anyone taking medication of any kind should not also drink alcohol.

Brief Interventions

The outstanding success of alcohol intervention research is 'brief interventions'. The groundbreaking study was counterintuitive and conducted in London around 40 years ago. A short intervention consisting of an assessment of drinking and brief advice was compared with the full programme of an alcohol treatment unit consisting of medical care, individual and group therapy, and social work support. At the end of treatment there were no differences between the two approaches. This research revolutionised the approach to treating alcohol problems. In the United States a tool called the 'drinkers checkup' was developed. This consisted of a detailed interview and tests all conducted in a single session. Later, this evolved to the FRAMES approach, which was based on a mixture of giving information and personalised feedback couched in a motivational interview style of counselling. The components are:

F   feedback — assessment and evaluation of the problem

R   responsibility — emphasising that drinking is by choice

A   advice — explicit advice on changing drinking behaviour

M   menu — offering alternative goals and strategies

E   empathy — the role of counsellor is important

S   self-efficacy — instilling optimism that the chosen goals can be achieved

FRAMES style interventions have been evaluated in many kinds of health settings including GP surgeries, hospital wards and accident-and-emergency departments. There is now a vast body of research showing that they are very effecting in helping people to significantly reduce their drinking from hazardous to safer levels. The problem, however, is that although these interventions are very effective not many people have access to this kind of help. For a variety of reasons, doctors have sometimes been reluctant to include brief interventions about alcohol in their consultations.

The lack of availability had led to the search for other ways to make them available. There have been some attempts to offer help via newspapers, magazines and computers (which had a reasonable amount of success), but the advent of the internet has enabled a new range of possibilities. When brief interventions have been adapted for the internet and provided to students, they have been extremely successful. Mostly these interventions have concentrated on self-assessments and feedback. Longer computerised interventions have also been developed for the internet in the US, Holland and Britain. The Dutch version was provided to people wanting alcohol treatment and was very successful. The British version was made available to anyone looking for help on the internet. The study used Down Your Drink which was the programme that formed the original basis for the material in this book. For this reason, we will give this study a bit more attention.

Down Your Drink was developed from a self-help programme written by alcohol counsellors, psychologists, health educators and individuals who had previously had drinking problems themselves. The original version was in a printed format and sent to people through the post in six weekly parts. The internet version included all the material from the printed edition plus much more. There was lots of pilot work with thousands of people using it and some of them gave feedback on how to improve the site. The research study was a randomized controlled trial comparing the interactive version of Down Your Drink with a version that had similar information, but was less interactive — more like an ordinary information-only website. Nearly 8000 people took part in the study and in both groups there were large reductions in consumption. This was from an average of 46 units a week at the beginning (before using the programme) to an average of 23 units a week after 12 months. The reduction happening in both groups was not something that was expected; it was probably due to the method of recruitment. All the participants were people who had been looking for help and, therefore, likely to be highly motivated to change anyway.

Conclusion — What Is the Research Telling Us?

The primary and most important conclusion from research is that changing habitual and harmful drinking is possible and many people have achieved it. The majority of the treatment research has been conducted with people whose drinking has been heavy and worrying enough for them to be part of services for dependence. The exception is the research on brief interventions, which has included a far wider range of people and settings. Transferring the conclusions from this research to people who are not dependent or approaching dependence is a bit of a stretch, but useful to attempt if this will give us some helpful guidance.

The strength of the evidence for brief interventions is significant and it is undoubtedly worthwhile to make sure that these interventions are made as widely available as possible in many settings. If people come across the opportunity to quickly evaluate their drinking and get some advice, then this might be enough to start them on their journey. Once begun, the journey is most probably helped by an approach that incorporates the principles of motivational interviewing. In this way an individual can set a personal and well-thought-out goal for themselves. To actually make some changes to drinking, the very practical approach of cognitive behaviour therapy and controlled drinking makes the most sense. Once a change has been made then relapse prevention helps to keep a person on track, sticking to their goals and overcoming problems as they come along.

The approach in this book has been to follow these research conclusions as far as possible. There is a great value in research, but there is also an important limitation to keep in mind. The data collected from randomized controlled trials (the dominant approach in this field) tells us what groups of people do in the conditions in which the trial was conducted. It does not tell us much about what any particular individual will do and it does not tell us what happens in circumstances that are somewhat different from the conditions in which the original research was conducted. So research of this type can give guidance but not definitive rules; there will always be individual differences. Therapists and counsellors know this, so they adapt the treatments they use to meet the needs of the individuals they are trying to help. There is an art to therapy and an art to interpreting science. You will need to develop some art yourself to make best use of the ideas in this book.

A Few References

This is not an academic book, but for those who would like to follow up some of the research themselves a few key references are listed below:

Heather, N., and Robertson, I. (1983) *Controlled Drinking*. London: Taylor & Francis.

Kaner, E. F. S., et al (2007) 'Effectiveness of Brief Alcohol Interventions in Primary Care Populations (Review)'. Cochrane Database of Systematic Reviews, (2), CD004148

Linke S., McCambridge J., Khadjesari Z., Wallace P., and Murray E. (2008) 'Development of a Psychologically Enhanced Interactive Online Intervention for Hazardous Drinking'. *Alcohol and Alcoholism*, November 2008, 43(6): 669–74.

National Institute of Health and Clinical Excellence (2010) 'Alcohol-use Disorders: Preventing the Development of Hazardous and Harmful Drinking'. London: National Institute of Health and Clinical Excellence 2010. Report No.: PH24.

Project MATCH Research Group (1993). 'Project MATCH: Rationale and Methods for a Multisite Clinical Trial Matching Patients to Alcoholism Treatment'. *Alcoholism: Clinical and Experimental Research 17,* 1130–1145.

Raistrick, D., Heather, N., and Godfrey, C. (2006) 'Review of the Effectiveness of Treatment for Alcohol Problems'. National Treatment Agency for Substance Misuse.

UKATT research team (2005) 'Effectiveness of Treatment for Alcohol Problems: Findings of the Randomised UK Alcohol Treatment Trial (UKATT)'. *British Medical Journal 2005,* 331: 541.

Wallace P., Murray E., McCambridge J., et al. (2011) 'On-line Randomized Controlled Trial of an Internet Based Psychologically Enhanced Intervention for People with Hazardous Alcohol Consumption'. *PLoS One* 2011 (March 9), 6 (3): e14740.

Further Resources

The aim of this book has been to try to help you become more independent of alcohol and to give you some tools to reduce any harm you may have been experiencing from drinking. However, we recognise that you may need some more help than contained in this book, so we have listed some resources that you could find useful. When you are looking for further help you will have to form your own judgment about whether a particular organisation is the right one for you. Do they seem to be honest, professional, impartial, etc? If you are looking for counselling then you should check out the qualifications of the counsellors or therapists. Also check if they are registered with an appropriate professional organisation and have a code of good practice that they follow.

Most of the help available is for people who have problems with alcohol addiction and for their families. So they may not apply to all the readers of this book. But even if you are not addicted or dependent on alcohol you might still find them useful sources of information.

The organisations listed below are not being specifically recommended; we are simply telling you about them. Quite often organisations come and go and change, so while we have tried to ensure the contact details are up to date, it is best if you check them out yourself.

List of Organisations

Action on Addiction

www.actiononaddiction.org.uk / tel: 0845 126 4130.
This organisation takes action to disarm addiction through its research, treatment, family support, education and training.

Addaction

www.addaction.org.uk
UK-wide treatment agency, helping individuals, families and communities to manage the effects of drug and alcohol misuse.

Adfam

www.adfam.org.uk / tel: 020 7553 7640

Information and advice for families of alcohol and drug users. The website has a list of local family support services.

Alcoholics Anonymous Great Britain

www.alcoholics-anonymous.org.uk

The British branch of this worldwide network, AA is an organisation of men and women who share their experience with each other hoping to solve their problems and help others to recover from alcoholism.

Al-Anon

www.al-anonuk.org.uk / tel: 0207 40 30 888

Al-Anon is worldwide and offers support and understanding to the families and friends of problem drinkers, whether the alcoholic is still drinking or not.

Alcohol Concern

www.alcoholconcern.org.uk / tel: 0207 566 9800

National agency on alcohol misuse campaigning for effective alcohol policy and improved services for people whose lives are affected by alcohol-related problems. There is a treatment service directory found at servicesdirectory.alcoholconcern.org.uk

Alcohol Focus Scotland

www.alcohol-focus-scotland.org.uk / tel: 0141 572 6700

Scotland's national voluntary organisation. Provides information and advice on responsible drinking.

Alcohol Help Centre

www.alcoholhelpcenter.net

Free, evidence-based behaviour change website aimed at helping you cut down.

APAS

www.apas.org.uk

Independent provider of all kinds of services designed to reduce the harm alcohol causes to individuals, families and the communities they live in.

Aquarius

www.aquarius.org.uk
  Leading provider of alcohol and other addiction services.

ARP

www.arp-uk.org
  Offers holistic treatment and support to people with problematic alcohol and drug use, their carers and families.

Centre for Addiction and Mental Health (CAMH)

www.camh.net
  CAMH has created materials to help clients and their families, professionals and the general public learn more about addiction and mental health issues.

DrinkAware

www.drinkaware.co.uk
  Aims to increase awareness and understanding of the role of alcohol in society, enabling individuals to make informed choices about their drinking.

Drinker's Check-up

www.drinkerscheckup.com
  To help someone develop a better understanding of their drinking including any risks (e.g., to health) it could pose, whether they might want to change their drinking, and understand the ways you could change if you decide to.

Drinkline

Tel: 0800 917 8282 (open 24 hours)
  A free helpline, in complete confidence, for anyone worried about their own or someone else's drinking. They have details of local alcohol advice centres for help and advice.

Drug and Alcohol Service for London (DASL)

www.alcoholeast.org.uk DASL is a London based charity that helps communities to tackle the problems caused by drug and alcohol misuse.

Moderation Management

www.moderation.org

Moderation Management (MM) is a behavioural change program and national support group network for people concerned about their drinking and who desire to make positive lifestyle changes.

NHS Choices — Know Your Units

units.nhs.uk

This site provides advice and information on alcohol units, and how alcohol affects the body. It is the home of the DrinkCheck tool which enables you to assess your drinking.

Samaritans

www.samaritans.org / tel : 08457 90 90 90

Samaritans provides confidential non-judgemental emotional support, 24 hours a day for people who are experiencing feelings of distress or despair.

Smart Recovery UK

www.smartrecovery.org.uk

SMART Recovery supports individuals who want to abstain from any type of addictive behaviour or activity

The Recovery Network (TRN)

www.trntv.co.uk/addictions/alcohol

An area of this online social networking community website is dedicated to helping and supporting people affected by alcohol addiction. Members are able to remain anonymous and join online discussion forums, post video or text blogs, use the chat rooms either via voice, webcam or text.

Index